Local and Central Government

Kathleen Allsop

Hutchinson

London   Melbourne   Sydney   Auckland   Johannesburg

Hutchinson & Co. (Publishers) Ltd

An imprint of the Hutchinson Publishing Group

17–21 Conway Street, London W1P 5HL

Hutchinson Group (Australia) Pty Ltd
30–32 Cremorne Street, Richmond South, Victoria 3121
PO Box 151, Broadway, New South Wales 2007

Hutchinson Group (NZ) Ltd
32–34 View Road, PO Box 40–086, Glenfield, Auckland 10

Hutchinson Group (SA) (Pty) Ltd
PO Box 337, Bergvlei 2012, South Africa

First published 1976
Second edition 1978
Third edition 1982
© Kathleen Allsop 1976 and 1978
New material © Tom Brennan 1982

Set in IBM Press Roman
by Tek-Art Ltd, London SE25
Printed in Great Britain by The Anchor Press Ltd
and bound by Wm Brendon and Son Ltd
both of Tiptree, Essex

British Library Cataloguing in Publication Data

Allsop, Kathleen
  Local and central government.—3rd ed.
  1. Local government—Great Britain
  2. Great Britain—Politics and
  government—1964-
  I. Title II. Brennan, Tom
  352.041   JS3095

ISBN 0 09 147011 0

Contents

Acknowledgements

The author and publisher are grateful to the following for their permission to reproduce illustrations as indicated:

Bradford Metropolitan Council: pp. 10, 31, 46; Bradford *Telegraph and Argus*: pp. 52, 53, 124; British Rail, LM Region: p. 61; British Steel Corporation: p. 61; Camera Press: p. 56; Central Electricity Generating Board: p. 61; Central Office of Information: pp. 84, 107; Cheshire County Council: p. 13; Civil Service Commission (Crown Copyright): p. 118; Conservative & Unionist Central Office: pp. 77, 107; Controller of Her Majesty's Stationery Office (Crown Copyright): pp. 25, 92, 96, 99, 111; *Daily Mirror*: p. 15; Fox Photos: p. 9; Greater London Council: p. 29; *Guardian*: p. 80; Hawker Siddeley Dynamics Ltd. (for photo montage incorporating Minitram): p. 14; Keystone Press Agency: pp. 17, 87, 91, 94, 107, 108, 122; Labour Party: pp. 76, 79, 84, 107; *Labour Weekly*: p. 83; Liberal Party: p. 76; London Borough of Camden: p. 30; National Coal Board: p. 61; National Monuments Record: p. 114; Plaid Cymru: p. 62; Post Office: p. 61; Press Association: pp. 58, 89; *Public Service* (NALGO journal) and the individuals concerned: p. 40; Royal Aircraft Establishment (Crown Copyright): p. 118; Scottish National Party: p. 62; Shell International Petroleum Company Ltd.: p. 125; Shelter: p. 72; South East Thames Regional Health Authority: p. 56; *Sunday People*: p. 86; Unicef/Adrian Clark: p. 73; Vivienne Studios: p. 107; West Midlands County Council: p. 12; West Yorkshire Metropolitan Police: p. 16.

We are also grateful to the following for their permission to reproduce the tables and diagrams on the following pages:

P. Gordon Walker and Jonathan Cape Ltd.: p. 103; Controller of Her Majesty's Stationery Office (Crown Copyright): pp. 33, 45, 59, 66, 68, 69, 70, 115, 117, 120, *Guardian*: p. 20; GLC: p. 29; House of Commons: p. 90; Labour Party: p. 23; *Labour Weekly*: p. 20; Macmillan: pp. 83, 87; *Sunday Times*: p. 12.

Cartoons on pp. 5, 6, 14, 86, 95, 126 by Richard Moon; p. 28 by Osbert Lancaster; p. 80 by Les Gibbard.

Author's acknowledgements

I am very grateful to Councillor Tom Megahy, Councillor Eric Armitage, Frank Allaun M.P., Rt Hon. Reg Prentice M.P., and to my former colleagues Arthur Shearsby and Selwyn Akal, for their help with this book. None of them is responsible for what I have written. I am also indebted to the efficient and anonymous staff of Bradford Central Library and Information Office who helped me to find a lot of the information.

Chapter 1
The Smiths and public services

Imagine an ordinary family, living in a council house on the outskirts of an industrial town. Jack Smith, the father, is thirty-nine years old and works as a skilled fitter at a local engineering firm. His wife Margaret is thirty-six; she is a housewife and also has a part-time job on Fridays and Saturdays as a shop assistant. They have two children: Elizabeth, aged fourteen, and three-year-old Jimmy. A year ago Mrs Smith's father died. Her widowed mother, Mrs Jones, could not stand the loneliness and came to live with them.

Like most people, the Smiths use public services provided by their local councils, regional authorities, public corporations and government departments, every day of the week. Suppose they need these services more than usual on a day in September.

6.40 a.m.	Mrs Smith gets up first, goes to the bathroom and notices that the water-tap is dripping and the W.C. water-tank is leaking slightly. She prepares breakfast for the family, using a gas cooker, and stokes the kitchen boiler with coke.
7.40 a.m.	Jack Smith catches a bus to work.
8.40 a.m.	Elizabeth dashes off to school at the last minute and nearly trips over part of the road which is being re-surfaced.
9 a.m.	Mrs Smith and her mother begin the housework, using an electric washing machine and vacuum cleaner.
9.30 a.m.	The postman delivers an electoral registration form and a letter from Mrs Smith's brother, a sergeant in the Army.
10.30 a.m.	Dustmen clear away the refuse.
11 a.m.	Mrs Jones goes to the post office to draw her pension. She notices that builders have started work on a new supermarket, for which the local council gave planning permission last year.
11.25 a.m.	Elizabeth's class at school watches a BBC television programme.
2 p.m.	Mrs Smith takes Jimmy to the clinic, then calls at the local council's branch office to report the leaks in the bathroom. They return through the park, where Jimmy has a go on the swings.
3 p.m.	Mrs Jones goes to a meeting of the Pensioners' Club at the new Community Centre, recently opened by the local council.
5 p.m.	Elizabeth returns home late, after calling at the public library to collect some information for a school project.
5.15 p.m.	Mr Smith returns from work and the family sit down together for their evening meal.
6 p.m.	Elizabeth goes to the Youth Centre with her friend Sally, who lives with foster-parents.
6.15 p.m.	Mr Smith sets off to collect some vegetables from his allotment, taking a short cut through the cemetery and over the railway bridge. He finds his tool-shed on fire;

the man on the next allotment has already called the fire-brigade and the police. The fire is soon put out, but several tools are missing and the policeman takes down particulars.

7 p.m.   Elizabeth comes home early, feeling ill, and is violently sick several times. Her mother telephones the doctor from a call-box. When the doctor arrives he suspects food poisoning and takes away the remains of a meat pie which Elizabeth has eaten, for testing by the Public Analyst.

9 p.m.   More bad news. Mr Smith tells his wife that there are strong rumours at work of a take-over by a big engineering group, which might mean the sack for some of them. He decides to call at the Jobcentre next day to enquire about local vacancies in his trade.

How many public services are mentioned in the above account? (There are at least thirty-two and the answers are given below.) How many public services did you use yesterday?

Answers

Water, W.C. (sewage), gas, coke, bus, school, road, electricity, post, electoral registration form, Army, dustmen, pension, council planning, BBC, clinic, council house repairs, park, swings, Community Centre, library, Youth Centre, foster-parents, allotment, cemetery, railway, fire-brigade, police, call-box, doctor, Public Analyst, Employment Office.

Chapter 2
Local government services

The Smiths used at least eighteen services provided by their district and county councils. The chart below shows the national picture. You could borrow a rate bill to find out which services are run by your local councils. In London the services are divided differently.

Your at-a-glance guide to who looks after what

	If you live in a Metropolitan County Greater Manchester (1) Merseyside (2) South Yorkshire (3) Tyne and Wear (4) West Midlands (5) West Yorkshire (6)		If you live in a Non-Metropolitan County	
	District Council	*County Council*	*District Council*	*County Council*
Large-scale planning Roads and traffic Road safety Parking Highway lighting Police* Fire service		●		●
Education Personal social services Careers Libraries	●			●

Local plans
Planning applications
Housing
House improvement grants
Slum clearance
Environmental health
   e.g. Dangerous structures
   Rodent control
   Food safety and hygiene
   Street cleansing
   Shops
   Home safety
   Communicable diseases
Refuse collection
Rent rebates
Rates and rate rebates
	●		●	

Off-street parking Parks, playing fields and open spaces Museums and art galleries Swimming baths	These are facilities which may be provided be either county or district according to local decision.			

*Controlled by a special authority of the County Council and the magistrates.

Local councils get their powers from Acts of Parliament, which make certain services, such as education, 'mandatory' (compulsory). Other powers are 'permissive'—a council can please itself whether it provides museums, art galleries, swimming baths. If a council wants to do something which is not allowed by general Acts it may be able to get special permission by a Private Act of Parliament.

The services listed on the chart are free at the time you use them, or make small charges a long way below the real cost. Some councils also run 'trading services' for which people pay the full cost when they use them—buses, markets, slaughterhouses, crematoria, race-courses. Can you think of any others?

In a short book it is impossible to describe all local government services. The brief notes below concentrate on the main ones.

Education

The councils of non-metropolitan counties, metropolitan districts, and outer London boroughs are 'Local Education Authorities'. (The Inner London boroughs form a joint Inner London Education Authority.) They are responsible for providing enough school places, and also for nursery and special schools, colleges of further education, and leisure facilities.

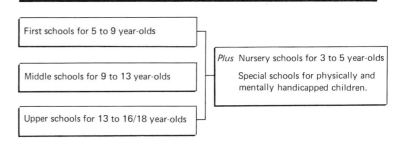

A 'three-tier' pattern of LEA schools. This pattern is used in some districts. How is it different where you live?

You could make a survey of the educational services in your own area.

☐ How many infant, junior and secondary schools are there? Or have your schools been reorganized in a 'three-tier' pattern (see diagram) or with Sixth Form Colleges? Do some of the schools select pupils by examinations, or is there a completely comprehensive system?

☐ How many schools are owned by churches, but have their running costs paid by the councils?

☐ How many nursery schools are there? What are the local rules for admitting children under five? What are the arguments for providing more nursery school places?

☐ How many special schools are there for handicapped children?

☐ How many young workers under eighteen attend day-release courses at your colleges of further education? Should it be compulsory for all young workers to spend one day a week at college, to learn more about their jobs and to improve their general education? What other courses do the colleges provide?

☐ Do the local governors or managers of schools include representatives of parents and pupils?

☐ What leisure facilities does the council provide?

☐ If you were a member of the council's Education Committee what improvements would you propose in the local system?

A special school for deaf children in London

Housing

District councils play a big part in tackling the main housing problems—the overall shortage of houses and flats, the unhealthy or out-of-date condition of something like five-million homes, and actual homelessness of families.

Local councils have built about six-million new houses and flats since 1920. Big estates, high-rise flats, maisonettes, bungalows for the elderly—what has your council built?

Slum clearance is a never-ending problem because houses wear out, especially if they were jerry-built in the first place. About two-thirds of the houses which are 'unfit for human habitation' are owned by private landlords. Councils have powers to buy property by 'compulsory purchase' and also to close or demolish unfit houses. The owners have a legal right to compensation and to object. The tenants are usually delighted to be rehoused by the council in modern homes. But they sometimes miss their old familiar community, swept away by bulldozers.

How many new houses and flats? (England and Wales) 1969-79

Year	Local Councils and New Towns	For Private Owners	Others*	Total
1969	139 850	173 377	10 938	324 165
1970	134 874	162 084	10 308	307 266
1971	117 215	179 998	12 563	309 776
1972	93 635	184 622	9 037	287 294
1973	79 289	174 413	10 345	264 047
1974	99 423	129 626	12 124	241 173
1975	122 857	140 381	15 456	278 694
1976	124 152	138 477	16 031	278 660
1977	121 246	128 127	26 041	275 414
1978	96 752	134 142	22 576	253 470
1979	74 952	119 520	17 797	212 269

*Includes certain housing associations and houses/flats for police, prison staff, H.M. Forces and so on.
(*Source: Annual Abstract of Statistics*)

You will get a clearer picture if you turn these figures into a graph or bar diagram. How do you account for the falling numbers?

Should councils concentrate more on the improvement of out-of-date houses? They already pay out improvement grants. The 'standard grant' helps owners of old houses to install hot-water systems, fixed baths, sinks and wash basins, and inside toilets.

Barkerend Improvement Area, Bradford: Before . . . and After

Councils have the power to improve whole run-down areas with trees, shrubs and play areas, as well as by modernizing the houses.

To what extent should councils help people who want to buy a house? They provide some loans for people who cannot get or afford a mortgage from a building society. A few councils have built houses specially to sell. Others help housing associations and 'build-it-yourself' groups.

The Housing Act 1980 gave council tenants who have lived in their houses for three years the right to buy their home. Some councils are not happy about this. Why?

The cost of building all kinds of houses shoots up if development land is expensive. This is a national problem for the Government to tackle.

Is it easy or difficult to rent or buy a house in your district?

Environmental health

These services prevent disease and help to keep our surroundings healthy.

Food, drink and drugs

Public Analysts and Public Health Inspectors investigate unsound food and drink. The inspectors take regular samples from shops, restaurants, slaughterhouses and farms, as well as dealing with complaints from doctors and the public.

Clean air

Smoke control areas have done a lot to get rid of smoke pollution. But some places still suffer from industrial pollution by grit and dust, sulphur and lead. Environmental Health Officers have powers to control it, and also the growing problem of noise pollution. If you live in a polluted district you may well wonder if their powers are strong enough.

Buildings

Councils lay down minimum standards of space, light, ventilation, sanitation and drainage for all new buildings. Public Health Inspectors report unfit houses for repair or demolition. They investigate smelly drains and 'offensive trades' such as maggot farms, and send Pest Control Officers to get rid of bugs, lice and rats.

Refuse

What happens to the fourteen million tons of refuse a year, collected by dustmen? Does your council dump it on tips or burn it in incinerators? Nottingham City Council uses part of the rubbish to heat the houses on a council estate.

Street cleansing

What kind of machines and how many men does your council employ on this job?

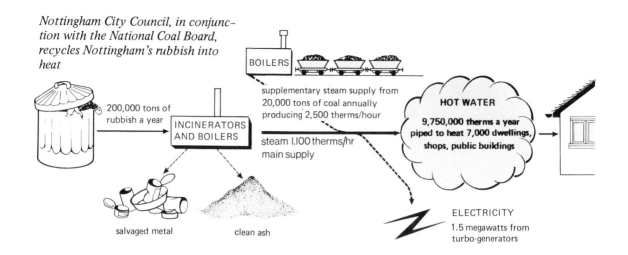

Nottingham City Council, in conjunction with the National Coal Board, recycles Nottingham's rubbish into heat

BOILERS

200,000 tons of rubbish a year

INCINERATORS AND BOILERS

supplementary steam supply from 20,000 tons of coal annually producing 2,500 therms/hour

steam 1,100 therms/hr main supply

salvaged metal

clean ash

HOT WATER

9,750,000 therms a year piped to heat 7,000 dwellings, shops, public buildings

ELECTRICITY
1.5 megawatts from turbo-generators

Consumer protection

Trading Standards Inspectors, employed by county councils, regularly test scales and so on to make sure that customers get the full amount they have paid for. They can also chase traders who give misleading descriptions of goods and services, or sell expensive goods which rapidly fall to pieces.

Has your county council set up any 'Consumer Advice Centres'? These centres give pre-shopping advice and information, in addition to dealing with complaints from unlucky customers.

A Consumer Advice Centre in Birmingham

Social services

Local councils help people in need, especially the elderly, physically and mentally handicapped, children, and families with serious problems.

12

The Chairman of a Social Services Committee put it like this:

'We never have enough money to do the job properly. There aren't enough trained social workers or staff willing to work in residential homes for the elderly and handicapped.

We don't put people into residential homes if we can help it. So we provide a home help service, meals-on-wheels, day centres, council bungalows and flats with a warden nearby. If we had more hostels, training centres and workshops, more mentally handicapped people could leave the hospitals.

The Chronically Sick and Disabled Persons Act, 1970, tells us to help such people by altering doors for wheelchairs, installing telephones and so on. Do we do enough?

Most of the children in our care have parents who can't look after them. Sometimes it's temporary, because the mother is in hospital. We've found foster-parents for half the children in care; the other half are in our residential nurseries or homes with housemothers. Should more use be made of adoption?

Our social workers help families whose worries have got on top of them and mothers who struggle alone.

Our services would collapse without the help of voluntary organizations—Women's Royal Voluntary Service, Red Cross, National Society for the Prevention of Cruelty to Children, church societies and many more. The council helps them financially, especially for running residential homes.'

Does your council have similar problems?

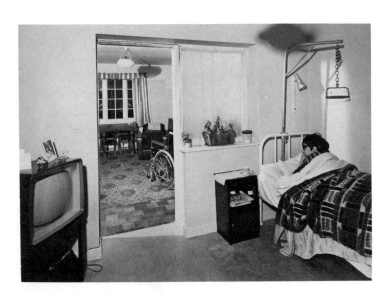

A disabled boy's home: how many special features can you spot which should make life easier for him?

Roads and traffic

County councils are responsible for most roads and bridges, road safety, highway lighting, traffic regulations and parking. (Motorways are the direct responsibility of central government.)

13

Our roads have never caught up with the rapid increase of motor transport. Should we spend more public money on roads? Or try to limit the use of cars and lorries, especially in town centres?

Public Transport

All county councils have power 'to promote the provision of a co-ordinated and efficient system of public passenger transport.' Some counties run their own bus services, side by side with the National Bus Company and private firms. British Rail is a separate public corporation.

Shall we go shopping in the future by automatic guideways?

In 1979 the Greater London Council introduced a system of cheap public transport which was subsidised from the rates. But this ran into legal difficulties and was deemed to be unlawful.

The West Midlands County Council and South Yorkshire County Council also adopted cheap fare policies but these may have to be scrapped because of the decision on London.

Some people argue that better and cheaper bus services would win passengers back from private cars, help to cure traffic congestion, and save money on roads. Bus fares have risen steeply because fewer passengers have paid for higher costs. A few councils introduced 'cheap fares' schemes but these caused great controversy and ran into legal difficulties (see opposite).

A few councils favour light rail schemes or new underground railways, able to carry up to 30 000 passengers an hour in heavily-populated areas. Perhaps we shall travel one day on automatic guideways, electronically controlled by computers?

Whatever the method, should public transport be run on commercial lines, or subsidized by taxes and rates to keep fares low, or even free for some people? What improvements in local transport services would you suggest to your county council?

Planning

The aim of planning is to make an area a better place for people to live, work and play. But plans to build new factories, which will create new jobs, may at the same time spoil the landscape. Plans to modernize a town centre may hurt individuals whose homes are demolished.

County and district councils are planning authorities. They have negative powers to refuse planning permission for new development. This applies to a house-owner who wants to build a garage, as well as

The couple with a view they call 'Hell':
Public reaction in London to motor-
way constructions.
   The anger shows . . . in a banner

to a powerful company which has its eye on a beauty spot for a new oil refinery. Fees for planning permission were introduced for the first time in 1980.

Councils have a positive duty to prepare their own plans for future development. County councils draw up broad 'structure plans'. District councils are responsible for 'local plans', fitting into the county plans and giving details of proposed changes. All councils must publicize their plans before they make final decisions.

Individuals or groups who object, especially if the plans involve compulsory purchase of their property, can appeal to the Department of Environment. If they have a reasonable case, the Minister orders an inquiry by one of his inspectors. He then decides in favour of the council or of the objectors.

The Lord Chancellor, *not* the Department of Environment, now appoints independent inspectors to hold public inquiries into major new road plans. This change followed the breakdown of several inquiries in 1976-7.

Have you read anything recently in local newspapers about your councils' plans and objections to them?

Police

Keeping law and order is the oldest function of government. Every citizen still has the right to arrest anybody 'caught in the act', a relic of the days when police forces did not exist.

In London the Metropolitan Police come directly under the Home Office. Elsewhere police forces are maintained by single or combined counties. Each 'police authority' sets up a joint committee (two-thirds councillors and one-third magistrates) which appoints the Chief Constable. He directs and controls the police force and submits an annual report. The committee cannot give him orders, but it can bring about his 'retirement'.

Crime prevention and detection are the most publicized duties of the police. From personal observation you can probably make a list of the other things they do.

Fire services

Each county council runs its own fire service, but the brigades help one another when big fires break out. Firemen give advice on fire prevention and escape, as well as fighting fires—a job made even more dangerous by modern plastics and chemicals.

Have you ever called a fire brigade to rescue a cat stuck in a tree or a small boy jammed in a hole? If so, did they make a charge for these non-fire services, as they are allowed to do?

Finding out about local government services

Many councils have information offices which supply free leaflets, pictures and diagrams about their services. Local newspapers publish reports and feature articles. You could organize a wall newspaper,

16

Firemen fighting the blaze at
Flixborough chemical plant

using one sheet for each service. Or collect material for a folder about one service. You may be able to interview a councillor or people employed by the council and write up your own report.

Chapter 3
The structure of local government

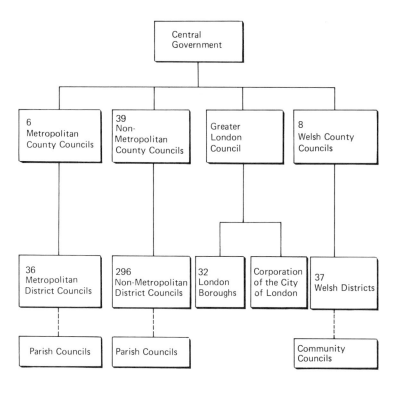

The structure of local government

In April 1974, the structure of local government in England and Wales (outside London) was transformed. No wonder the previous system had got out-of-date; it was set up in the late nineteenth century, an era of gas lamps and horse-drawn trams.

After years of inquiries and debates Parliament passed the Local Government Act, 1972, which set up the two-tier pattern of councils shown in the chart. The Act also shuffled the pack of local government services and re-dealt them to the new councils.

Every area now has two principal councils:

1 *County Councils:* the six metropolitan councils cover almost continuous urban areas; their total population is about nineteen-millions. The thirty-nine non-metropolitan county councils cover less densely populated areas; they have considerably more functions than the metropolitan county councils (see chart on p.7).
2 *District Councils:* the metropolitan district councils have more powers than the other districts. For example, they run education and social services, which are county functions elsewhere.

18

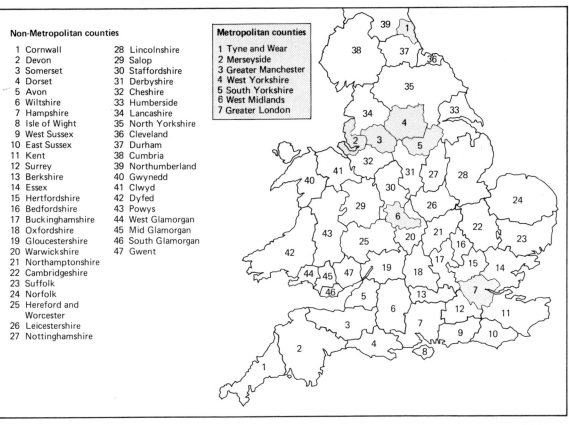

Non-Metropolitan counties

1 Cornwall
2 Devon
3 Somerset
4 Dorset
5 Avon
6 Wiltshire
7 Hampshire
8 Isle of Wight
9 West Sussex
10 East Sussex
11 Kent
12 Surrey
13 Berkshire
14 Essex
15 Hertfordshire
16 Bedfordshire
17 Buckinghamshire
18 Oxfordshire
19 Gloucestershire
20 Warwickshire
21 Northamptonshire
22 Cambridgeshire
23 Suffolk
24 Norfolk
25 Hereford and
   Worcester
26 Leicestershire
27 Nottinghamshire

28 Lincolnshire
29 Salop
30 Staffordshire
31 Derbyshire
32 Cheshire
33 Humberside
34 Lancashire
35 North Yorkshire
36 Cleveland
37 Durham
38 Cumbria
39 Northumberland
40 Gwynedd
41 Clwyd
42 Dyfed
43 Powys
44 West Glamorgan
45 Mid Glamorgan
46 South Glamorgan
47 Gwent

Metropolitan counties

1 Tyne and Wear
2 Merseyside
3 Greater Manchester
4 West Yorkshire
5 South Yorkshire
6 West Midlands
7 Greater London

Metropolitan and non-metropolitan counties in England and Wales

How does your area fit into this picture? The public library will have a map showing the boundaries of your county and the districts into which it is divided.

London

The London Government Act, 1963, reorganized London's system of local government earlier than the rest of England and Wales. The Greater London Council covers a population of about eight millions. The thirty-two London Boroughs are smaller in population than most of the metropolitan districts. Some of them may be joined together in the future to form bigger units.

Scotland

Scottish local government was reorganized in April, 1975, on different lines from England and Wales. It is a two-tier system of councils in nine regions, three island groups and fifty-three districts. Half the population live in the Strathclyde Region, which includes Glasgow.

19

Districts of Merseyside Metropolitan County

Map of London boroughs

1 Barking
2 Barnet
3 Bexley
4 Brent
5 Bromley
6 Camden
7 Croydon
8 Ealing
9 Enfield
10 Greenwich
11 Hackney
12 Hammersmith
13 Haringey
14 Harrow
15 Havering
16 Hillingdon
17 Hounslow
18 Islington
19 Kensington and Chelsea
20 Kingston-upon-Thames
21 Lambeth
22 Lewisham
23 Merton
24 Newham
25 Redbridge
26 Richmond-upon-Thames
27 Southwark
28 Sutton
29 Tower Hamlets
30 Waltham Forest
31 Wandsworth
32 Westminster

Co-operation between councils

Some local government functions overlap, notably planning and the provision of parks, playing fields, museums, art galleries and swimming baths. County and district councils can set up joint committees to deal with them.

Agency arrangements allow one council to run a service for which another council is legally responsible. For example, county councils are responsible for disposal of refuse, but they may allow district councils to do the job for them. You may find similar arrangements in your area for consumer protection, libraries and roads. But agency arrangements cannot be made for education, social services and police.

Parish and community councils

About 10 000 small towns and villages have parish councils (in England) or community councils (in Wales), in addition to their two principal councils. The Local Government Act, 1972, allowed existing parish councils and parish meetings in rural areas to continue. The Government also set up about 350 'successor' parish councils for some of the small towns which lost their old urban district or borough councils.

All these minor councils have limited powers to deal with parks and open spaces, footpaths, village halls, public lavatories, allotments, and to discuss planning applications. What they actually do varies from place to place; it depends partly on the attitude of the district council.

'An important criterion of a true neighbourhood council is the aim to be representative of and responsible to its community through an electoral procedure in which all of its people can take part.'

Some critics think that there should be similar urban parish or neighbourhood councils in big towns, 'where people can come with any gripe or groan, for instance a cracked pavement'. At the moment neighbourhood councils have no statutory (legal) status but the Department of the Environment has issued a circular setting out what they think is the best basis for these councils. (See left)

How has reorganization of local government worked out?

Good or bad, the new system will probably last for many years to come. Nobody wants another major upheaval in the near future.

Meanwhile criticism goes on, from irate citizens who found their rate bills shooting up alarmingly in 1974 and blamed the new system, and from councillors who never liked the two-tier arrangement. They say that the sharing of powers between county and district councils causes wrangles, arguments and delays.

Some critics say that the non-metropolitan districts are too small and weak for tackling big housing problems, and the counties too small for planning large-scale development. Other critics reply, 'No, they're too big and remote from the people they serve. People get confused and can't track down who is responsible for decisions which affect their lives.'

Defenders of the new system say that it fits our modern pattern of life much better than the old one. It links up town and country areas in districts. The new councils are bigger and fewer than the old ones, so they have more money to finance the services and better qualified staff to run them.

Have you heard any criticisms locally about the new system of councils?

Chapter 4
Local elections

When were local elections last held in your district and county? What were the results?

How often are local elections held?

It depends where you live. Elections are held every fourth year for county councils. Districts vary:

Metropolitan districts have elections every year, except when it is the year for the county council election.

All other districts can choose *either* to use the same system of electing one third of the councillors at a time, *or* to hold one election for the whole council every fourth year.

The table below shows the general pattern for some authorities and the possible variations for others. Which patterns are followed in your area?

Local election arrangements

(The normal day of election will be the first Thursday in May)

	3 May 1979 5 May 1983 7 May 1987 *etc.*	1 May 1980 3 May 1984 5 May 1988 *etc.*	7 May 1981 2 May 1985 4 May 1989 *etc.*	6 May 1982 1 May 1986 3 May 1990 *etc.*
County councils			Whole council	
Greater London Council			Whole council	
London borough councils				Whole council
Metropolitan district councils	$\frac{1}{3}$ council	$\frac{1}{3}$ council		$\frac{1}{3}$ council
Welsh district councils	$\frac{1}{3}$ council or whole council	$\frac{1}{3}$ council or none		$\frac{1}{3}$ council or none
Non-metropolitan district councils (England)	$\frac{1}{3}$ council or whole council	$\frac{1}{3}$ council or none		$\frac{1}{3}$ council or none
Parish councils in metropolitan districts	Whole council			
Parish councils in non-metropolitan districts	Whole council*	None*		None*
Community councils	Whole council*	None*		None*

* Where a Welsh district council or a non-metropolitan district council is elected by thirds, the year of parish or community council elections may be altered to coincide with the election of district councillors for the area in which the parish or community is located.

(*Source: Local Government Handbook: England and Wales, 1981*)

Who can vote at elections?

☐ Your name must be on the current register of electors.

☐ You must be a British subject, or a citizen of the Republic of Ireland.

☐ You must be eighteen or over on polling day.

Certain people are *disqualified* from voting—aliens, prisoners serving sentences of more than one year, and persons convicted of corrupt practices at elections. Peers (dukes, earls, barons) can vote at local elections but not at parliamentary ones.

Every autumn a local official, the Electoral Registration Officer, sends out forms to every household in his area. The head of each household has to write down the names of all adults who normally live there on 10 October. He can be fined up to £20 if he refuses or forgets to do this.

'Adults' include young people who are only seventeen on 10 October, or even only sixteen in a few cases. The head of the household puts their date of birth on the form, so that they will be able to vote at any election on or after their eighteenth birthday.

The Electoral Registration Officer publishes a provisional list of electors on 28 November. He sends copies to post offices and public libraries. Only eighteen days are allowed, up to 16 December, for people to check that their names are on the list. If not, they should quickly put in a claim. If they don't claim they will not be able to vote for a whole year at any election after 16 February, when the new register comes into force.

Three methods of voting

1 *Voting in person*

Most people vote at their local polling station. They get an official poll card which tells them where to go.

2 *Voting by post*

Thousands of people cannot vote in person. You can apply for a postal vote

(a) if the general nature of your work *may* prevent your voting in person. This covers people like long-distance lorry drivers, doctors, sales representatives and so on.

(b) if you *may* be prevented by 'physical incapacity'. This includes hospital patients and also sufferers from diseases like chronic bronchitis. You need the signature of a doctor, hospital matron or qualified nurse on this form.

You cannot apply for a postal vote if you are going to be away on holiday. People who have moved away from the district can get one for parliamentary elections but *not* for local elections.

3 *Voting by proxy*

Service men and women, crown servants working abroad, and certain civilians working at sea or abroad, can appoint somebody to vote for them.

The legal rules about postal and proxy votes are complicated and

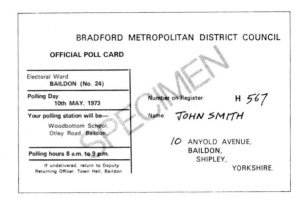

Official poll card

R.P.F.7

(*Please complete in block letters*)

(1) I, (*Surname*) ....

(*Other names*) ....
am qualified to be registered as an elector for (*address in full*)

....
....

(2) I apply to be treated as an absent voter at parliamentary and local government elections because I am likely to be unable to go in person to the polling station (or, where (c) or (d) below applies, to vote unaided)
   *(a) by reason of the general nature of my occupation, service or employment as

....
....
(*Give full reason for application*)
   *(b) by reason of the general nature of the occupation, service or employment of my *husband/wife as

....
and my resulting absence from my qualifying address until
.... (*insert likely date of return*)
to be with my *husband/wife
   *(c) by reason of blindness †(in respect of which I have been registered as a blind person by the

.... Council)
   *(d) by reason of physical incapacity (*see Note 2*)
Signed .... Date ....
Address in the United Kingdom to which ballot paper is to be sent (if different from address given above)

....
....

*Delete whichever is inapplicable.
†If the applicant is not registered as a blind person, the words in brackets should be deleted and the certificate or declaration on the back should be completed.

Application form for postal vote

only the main ones are given here. When in doubt ask the Electoral Registration Officer and check the last date for applications (about a fortnight before polling day).

Who can stand as a local candidate?

He or she must be a British subject, twenty-one years old or over, and have one of the following qualifications:

☐ Be included in the register of electors for the local government area.

☐ During the whole of the twelve months preceding his nomination have resided in the local government area.

☐ Have his principal or only place of work for twelve months within the area.

☐ Have for the whole of the previous twelve months occupied as owner or tenant any land or premises within the area.

He or she must *not* be an employee of the local authority concerned, a bankrupt, guilty of corrupt or illegal practices, or have been sent to prison for not less than three months within five years of an election.

Selection of candidates

Who selects the candidates in local elections? The Independents select themselves and have to pay their own election expenses. Anybody who has the legal qualifications can stand as a candidate, provided he can find ten local electors to sign his nomination paper.

The largest numbers of candidates are selected by the political parties to which they belong. The local parties draw up approved lists of candidates. In each ward or electoral division the party members (or a representative committee) pick out a few names from this list, invite them to speak at a party meeting, then vote for the one they like best.

In practice the approved list sometimes dwindles alarmingly, because people have removed or withdrawn after second thoughts.

This applies especially when one party is fighting a 'hopeless' seat or one it is not likely to win. Then the local party hastily looks round for suitable candidates not yet on the list and sometimes tells them, 'Don't worry, you're not likely to get in!'

Local political parties pay the election expenses and organize their members to publicize the candidate. If elected he will usually be expected to vote with his fellow party councillors.

Other candidates are selected by pressure groups, such as tenants' associations, ratepayers' associations, 'down-with-motorways' groups, etc. These groups spring up to keep the rents or rates down or to campaign for a particular issue. If elected the candidate may find that he or she is in a small minority on the council.

In many places political party candidates have a much better chance of election than independents. Can you think of any reason for this?

County Council elections 1981
(Results for 1977 and 1973 are given for comparison)

Year	Seats	Conservative	Labour	Liberal	Other	Vacancies
1981	4 367	1 732	1 860	393	376	4
1977	4 400	2 898	889	96	446	-
1973	4 400	1 638	1 849	262	641	10

What percentage of the total number of seats were won by party candidates in the three elections? Has this increased or decreased? How do you account for the gains and losses for each of the parties in successive elections?

A local election campaign

The candidate's first task is to write his election address, the traditional leaflet which tells the electors something about himself and the policies he supports. A party candidate usually writes only part of it; the rest is an agreed statement of policy from his district or county organization. What kind of an address would you write if you were a candidate, and what policies would you propose?

Every candidate must appoint an election agent to organize his campaign and look after legal formalities. He can share an agent with other candidates or even appoint himself. A party agent's report might read like this.

March 3   First meeting of ward election committee. We agreed to spend up to three-quarters of the legal maximum for 10 630 electors. (We are hard up.)
To aim at canvassing all 5000 houses, and try to find out where our supporters are.
To deliver the election address and 5000 leaflets from London H.Q. to every house.
To order posters, window bills and car stickers from a local printer.
March 13   Second meeting. We approved the candidate's draft of his election address and decided that canvassing teams should start four weeks before polling day.
March 16   I got the nomination and other legal forms from the

Returning Officer. The candidate helped me to collect electors' signatures.

April 9   Nomination Day. The candidate and I took the nomination papers and other forms to the Returning Officer at the council offices. As we expected, two other parties also nominated candidates.

April 30   Last meeting of ward election committee. We finalized our polling day arrangements. Canvass figures are not yet complete but they show a majority for our candidate if we can get our supporters out on polling day.'

Polling Day from three angles

The Voter

He usually takes his official poll card to the polling station, but he can vote without it. When he enters the polling station an official checks off his name and number on the electoral register. This prevents people voting twice. The voter is given a stamped ballot paper, showing the candidates' names and parties. He takes it to a booth and puts a cross against his choice, using a stubby pencil on a piece of string. He then folds the ballot paper and puts it in a sealed ballot box.

The Officials

The Returning Officer is responsible for legal forms and for organizing the polling stations. The presiding officer and clerks at each station work a long day, from 8 a.m. to 9 p.m. or even later if the count is held on the same evening. At 9 p.m. the presiding officer is responsible for getting the ballot boxes and the counterfoils of the ballot papers safely to the council offices, or wherever the count is held.

The Returning Officer or his deputy supervises the counting of the votes. First, the counting clerks make a straight count of the ballot papers; the total must be the same as the number of counterfoils. They are watched by hawk-eyed 'counting agents', appointed by the candidates. Then the counting clerks sort the ballot papers into piles for each candidate. The Returning Officer declares papers invalid if the voter's intention is not clear or if there is any writing on the paper. When all the votes have been added up the Returning Officer calls the candidates and agents together and quietly tells them the result. Then he announces the result publicly. You have probably seen this on television news.

The Candidate and his election workers

For the candidate and his agent it is an exhausting day. The agent directs his squad of volunteers: number-takers at the polling stations, who ask voters for their polling numbers; messengers who take the numbers back to the nearby 'committee room'; clerks in the committee rooms who cross off supporters who have voted; car drivers and 'knockers-up', who try to persuade supporters who have not voted to get out of their armchairs.

1	CHARLTON James Edward Charlton, 9 Midland Avenue, Banton Independent	
2	FLOOD John Flood, The Hollies, Oldwick Conservative	X
3	RENTON Glyn David Renton, 7 Acacia Grove, Banton Liberal	
4	WOODRIDGE Michael John Woodridge, 14 Hill Top Drive, Banton Labour	

Why is this ballot paper invalid?

27

At 9 p.m. the candidate, the agent and the 'counting agents' dash off to the count. Perhaps the agent sadly concludes his report like this. 'We lost by 206 votes so I didn't ask for a recount. We failed to get a lot of our supporters out to vote.'

Apathy?

Some seventy to eighty per cent of the electorate vote in general elections but usually only about half of this proportion turn out in local government elections. Why is there such an enormous difference? Local elections are not normally fought as vigorously as parliamentary elections and the publicity is not so great but this does not seem to be the only explanation for the lack of interest.

Some electors believe that who controls the local councils is not as important as which party controls the national government. Others consider that local elections should not be fought as a party battle. There is also evidence which shows that when many people do vote in local elections it is not *local* issues they have in mind but how they see the Government as performing *nationally*. In 1979 all district council elections, except in Scotland and London, were held on 3 May, the same day as the general election. On this occasion the turnout of voters for local election was nearly as high as that for the parliamentary election. It averaged 65 to 75 per cent, instead of the usual 35 to 45 per cent. How do you explain this?

'I've an awful feeling there's something we ought to be doing today, but I can't for the life of me remember what it is.'
(*From* Meaningful Confrontations, *Osbert Lancaster, John Murray*)

Chapter 5
How councils work

After the local elections the councillors are soon summoned to the first meeting of the new council. Have you ever attended a council meeting? It may be quite short or go on for hours with heated speeches about controversial proposals.

Council meetings

The Chamber where the council meets is usually semi-circular and members of the same party sit together in a group. The Chairman

Annual General Meeting of the Greater London Council

Plan of the Greater London Council Chamber
(Source: GLC pamphlet 'Procedure at Meetings', June 1977)

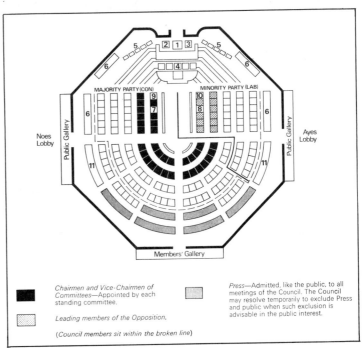

1 The Right Hon. the Chairman of the Council

2 The Vice-Chairman of the Council

3 The Deputy Chairman of the Council

4 The Director-General and Clerk to the Council

5 Distinguished visitors

6 Chief officers of departments of the Council's service

7 The Leader of the Council

8 The Leader of the Opposition

9 Chief Whip, Majority Party

10 Chief Whip, Minority Party

11 Senior officers of the departments

sits in the middle with the Chief Executive at his side. The Chief Executive is the principal paid official and he can speak but not vote. Below the platform sit committee clerks, who make an accurate record of the meeting. There are special galleries for the press and public.

Every council must hold an annual general meeting (AGM), normally in May. The first business is the election of a chairman and vice-chairman from among the councillors. The Chairman presides at meetings and he is also the ceremonial head in his district or county. He receives important visitors and attends a lot of local functions. In districts which have the status of boroughs he is called the Mayor or Lord Mayor.

A London Mayor (Camden) receiving Chinese visitors

How often do your councils meet? Councils make their own rules about that. The Chairman must call an 'extraordinary' meeting, in addition to the normal ones, if a certain number of councillors demand it. Each councillor gets a notice of meeting at least three clear days before the date, and a bulky packet of documents, including the minutes (record) of the last meeting and the agenda (list of matters to be dealt with) for the next meeting.

Most of the council's work is done in committees, but some of their decisions need the consent of a majority of the full council. The reports and recommendations are sometimes dealt with faster than you can read this sentence. A report is formally moved by the committee chairman, seconded, voted upon by a show of hands (or by pressing electric buttons), carried or defeated. If the voting is equal the Chairman of the council has a casting vote. Any councillor has the right to object to a committee recommendation and there may be a long debate.

There are special rules about resolutions which involve spending public money. If a councillor owns or has shares in a firm which might get a contract from the council, he must declare his financial

30

Agenda

1. **MINUTES**
   To authorise the Chairman to sign the minutes of the meeting held on 1st April 1974 as a correct record.

2. **ANNOUNCEMENTS**
   To receive announcements.

3. **PECUNIARY INTERESTS**
   To receive disclosures by members of any pecuniary interest.

4. **RECOMMENDATIONS OF COMMITTEES**
   (a)
   (i) To consider a recommendation of the Management Committee at their meeting on 30th April 1974.
   (The recommendation is set out on the blue page No. 3).

   (ii) To consider recommendations (if any) of the Management Committee at their meeting on 14th May 1974, relating to M650 Airedale Motorway.
   (The recommendations will be circulated at the meeting).

   (b) To consider a recommendation of the Educational Services Committee.
   (The recommendation is set out on the green page No. 5).

   (c) To consider a recommendation of the Development Services Committee.
   (The recommendation is set out on the pink page No. 9).

5. **MOTIONS BY MEMBERS**
   To consider the following motion of which notice has been given by Councillor Senior in accordance with Standing Order 9:-

   (a) That, notwithstanding any previous decision, the City of Bradford Metropolitan Council as a matter of policy seek the establishment of a Level 2 Joint County District Committee similar to those of the other four Metropolitan Districts; and

   (b) That delegation of responsibility be sought for various highway functions and that nominations for membership of this Joint Committee be discussed with the Party Whips forthwith.

6. **QUESTIONS**
   To deal with questions which do not relate to recommendations of Committees for consideration at this meeting of the Council in accordance with Standing Order 8.

7. **COMMENTS**
   To receive comments which do not relate to recommendations of Committees for consideration at this meeting of the Council in accordance with Standing Order 8(4) in Committee order as follows:-

   Management Committee
   Educational Services Committee
   Social Services Committee
   Development Services Committee

Agenda for City of Bradford Metropolitan Council meeting showing the normal order of business (except that on this particular day there were no petitions from the public)

interest. He can neither speak nor vote on the resolution. Any councillor who votes for a resolution to spend money outside the council's legal powers risks paying a surcharge or heavy fine out of his own pocket.

Standing orders

Every council draws up its own Standing Orders (rules of procedure) which the Chairman needs to know by heart.

Standing Orders lay down the rules of debate—how many times a member may speak and for how long. Some rules are common to all democratic bodies. For example, when a member has moved (proposed) a motion the Chairman says, 'Does anyone second this motion?' If somebody says, 'I second the motion', the member is allowed to speak in favour of it, followed by a general debate. If there is no seconder there is no discussion and no vote.

Standing Orders include a 'quorum' rule; for example, at least one-quarter of the members must be present or the meeting cannot be held. There are usually rules about committees—how membership is to be decided and how often they are to meet.

Powers of the council

Councils can delegate some of the powers they get from Parliament to their own committees, but only the full council can make decisions about rates (local taxes) and borrowing money.

A council can make its own bye-laws. These are local laws about minor matters on which Parliament has laid down the general principles. There is an Act which forbids school-children to do an unlimited amount of part-time paid work. Your school probably has a copy of the local bye-law about this. How many hours are you allowed to work during term-time and during the holidays?

Councils can also make minor regulations about their own services. 'Keep off the grass.' 'No parking.' 'This library will be open at the following hours . . . ' Can you think of any others?

Policy and administration

'The duty of local authority staffs is to give advice and carry out instructions. But it is the job of elected members to make policy.' That is the difference between paid officials and councillors.

In practice it is often difficult to draw a clear line between policy and administration. Suppose a council decides to provide more bus shelters (policy). The staff get on with the job and the shelters are built (administration). But the new shelters have fancy roofs which let the rain fall through on people's heads. Naturally the councillors get complaints and they are not likely to say, 'That's none of our business, we only deal with policy'.

On the other hand, some of the chief officers play a considerable part in making policy, through the advice and information which they give to councillors. They are not just paid servants to do as they are told.

Management structure

The main work of planning and running council services is done by committees of councillors and departments of paid staff.

A few years ago councils were criticized for setting up too many committees and sub-committees. They took up a great deal of councillors' time and sometimes went into minute details of administration. The Maud (Management) Report, 1967, quoted a committee where 'an architect's report gave the number of visits made to public conveniences for the purpose of carrying out repairs, which were itemized'.

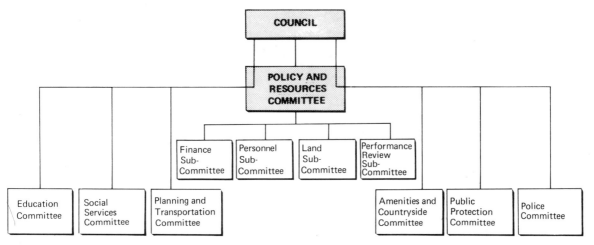

The committee structure of a non-metropolitan county

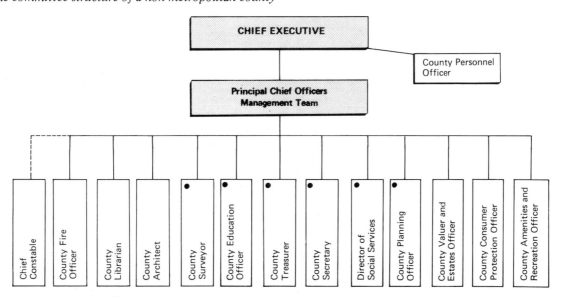

The departmental structure of a non-metropolitan county
(Source: The Bains Report, HMSO)

In some places departments had become almost like rival empires, with little co-operation between them. There is a story about a department which was instructed by the council to demolish some old buildings in a main street. The transport department of the same council blithely continued to run a bus service from the street, until waiting passengers complained loudly about falling lumps of masonry.

Something had to be done about these muddles and waste of time. The Bains Report, 1972, recommended

☐ a 'corporate' approach to council services—both councillors and officers should work as a team

☐ fewer council committees, which should concentrate on policy

☐ amalgamation of departments with related functions

☐ more delegation of administration to officers.

The diagrams on page 33 show some of the Bains Report suggestions about how the structure of committees and departments could be improved. You will probably find that your own councils arrange things differently. Each council decides its own management structure.

Council committees

You will find an Education Committee and a Social Services Committee on every list of county council (or metropolitan district) committees. These are 'statutory committees', compulsory by Act of Parliament.

Most councils have a central Policy and Resources (or Management) Committee of leading councillors, who try to look at the council's work as a whole. Their recommendations must go before a full council meeting, where every councillor has a chance to debate them. The Bains Report advised this central committee to set up sub-committees to look more closely at finance, manpower and land, and to review regularly the council's work.

Committees meet round a table and thrash things out together. At least one Chief Officer is present, ready to give information and advice. If something very important happens between committee meetings, the Chairman has emergency powers. Suppose an old people's home suddenly burns down. Which committee chairman would have to do some quick thinking?

The council decides how much freedom its committees shall have. They may be allowed to make their own decisions except on finance. Or they may be told to submit nearly all their proposals to the council meeting. Or something in between.

Any committee (except finance) may co-opt non-councillors, up to one-third of its total membership. These co-opted members take a full part in discussion and voting. The councillors generally choose people with useful knowledge and experience. But anybody who is disqualified from being a councillor is also disqualified from being appointed as a co-opted member.

34

All committees must allow the press and public to attend their meetings, unless they pass a special resolution to exclude them from a particular meeting. Can you think of any good reasons why they might do this?

Council departments

A large council employs 20 000 or more paid staff, organized in departments. Each department has a Chief or Principal Officer to manage it.

The Bains Report diagrams show a Chief Executive at the top of the tree, with a management team of four or five chief/principal officers. They work out together the advice they are going to give the council, and also try to avoid overlapping in administration. This is a fairly new idea. Some councils keep the older method of appointing a Clerk to the Council with less management power than a Chief Executive.

How does the list of department heads compare with your own council's arrangements?

Party politics in local government

Are your councils controlled by political parties or do they consist mostly of Independents? If you live in a big city, local elections have probably been fought on party lines for fifty years or more. If you live in a village, there may have been party contests for the first time in 1973. There is certainly a strong tendency for political parties to play an increasing role in local government.

Councillors who belong to the same party form a Party Group and elect their own Leader. The Group meets before full council meetings. They discuss the recommendations of council committees and decide what attitude they will take as a Group. This is where they hammer out differences of opinion within the party. If the Group has a clear majority on the council this is where the main issues of policy are decided.

Does a councillor always follow the party line at council meetings? Not necessarily. Each Group makes its own rules, hard or soft. But even if the rules are soft, a councillor who speaks or votes frequently against his party will probably find himself out on his ear at the next local election. If he wants to stand again it will be as an Independent.

People disagree about party politics in local government. Here is a summary of the main arguments:

Disadvantages of party control ?

Non-party candidates do not stand much chance of election, though they might make good councillors.

Politicians argue according to party doctrines, even if they are not relevant to particular local problems.

Party Groups make decisions, often in private, instead of at open council meetings.

35

Council debates suffer because of party hostilities.

Advantages of party control ?

Parties are based on political ideals, which give direction and purpose to council work.

Parties give the electors a choice of policies, not just of individuals.

They make it possible for people who cannot afford to pay their own election expenses to become councillors.

No individual councillor has all the talents and experience, but a party group can provide them as a team.

Can you think of any reason why country areas often have more Independent councillors than big cities?

Councillors and co-opted members — financial allowances and obligations

Authority for payment or requirement	Description	Details
Local Government Act 1972	Attendance Allowance	Payable to elected members only. Maxium allowance for 1974 was £10. This was raised to £11 in December 1977; to £12.14 in December 1978 and to £13.28 in December 1979. Most councils pay a lower rate for shorter periods
Local Government Act 1972	Financial Loss Allowance	Payable to those (e.g. co-opted members of a committee) who are not entitled to claim attendance allowance. Maximum to be claimed was raised to £14 in March 1980
Local Government, Planning and Land Act 1980	Travelling and Subsistence Allowances	The rates are fixed from time to time by the Secretary of State for the Environment
Local Government, Planning and Land Act 1980	Special Responsibility Allowance	Payable to members who have special responsibilities in the running of the Council
Local Government Act 1972	Declaration of Pecuniary Interest	Any member of the Council who has a pecuniary (i.e. financial) interest in any matter (e.g. a contract for building) being considered at a meeting when he or she is present must declare this. The member is normally excluded while the item is being considered. (See pages 31-2.)

Chapter 6
Councillors and council staff

A councillor's diary. How much time did the councillor spend on council work, party meetings, other duties?

The Robinson Committee of Inquiry reported that ordinary members spent on average 79 hours a month on council activities; committee chairmen, party leaders and mayors spend up to 122 hours a month. One-third of working councillors claimed that their attendance allowance was less than their loss of earnings. ('Remuneration of Councillors Report', Cmnd. 7010, 2 December 1977). Within the limits laid down (see table opposite), councils fix different scales of allowances. Some pay less than the maximum allowed and this may occasion hardship for individual councillors in the areas concerned.

What is it like to be a councillor?

The councillor opened his diary at a busy week in March. 'I do get a free evening sometimes, but it's often like this—council or party work every day.'

March 18 Monday	March 22 Friday
7 p.m. Party Group Meeting at Civic Hall, Room 101 (2hrs)	7:30 p.m. Public Meeting, national speaker (organised by Constituency party) at Glen Room (2hrs)
19 Tuesday	**23 Saturday**
4 p.m. Council Meeting at Civic Hall (2hrs)	2:30 p.m. Open Day, New Wrose Youth Centre (2hrs) 4:30 p.m. Visit Mrs Green (½hr.)
20 Wednesday	**24 Sunday**
4 p.m. Special Services sub-committee (Education) at Civic Hall, Room 12 (1½hrs)	aft. Correspondence, minutes, reports etc. (3hrs.)
21 Thursday	**NOTES**
2.45 p.m. N.E.Gas Consultative Council at Gas Board office. (1½hrs.)	Contact Social Services Dept. re. Mr. and Mrs. Pearson, 8. Albert St. (deaf child)

He was elected to a metropolitan district council in 1973, after eleven years' service on an urban district council. He works as a turner at a large engineering firm, which gives him time off (without pay) for council duties.

'We always hold our Party Group meeting in the evening before full council meetings. We thrash out any differences of opinion and decide who will speak for the party on each committee report. The other two parties hold their Group meetings on the same date.

We start council meetings at 4 p.m., as a compromise between day and evening meetings. It suits me, I don't have to leave work until three o'clock. We can claim an attendance allowance, when we're on official council business, up to £10 for 24 hours, plus necessary travelling expenses. I'm paid £5 for attending the council meeting. (See note on p. 37 and table opposite.)

I'm on the Social Services Committee, which meets every other month, and on its Residential Care sub-committee. There isn't much political argument—we're all keen to get the best services and the best staff for old and handicapped people and the children in care. We've visited several Homes and found out what improvements are needed, by talking to residents and the staff.

I'm also on the Special Services sub-committee (Education). This is a new system we've got, to link the work of the main committees together. This sub-committee covers the special schools for blind, deaf, crippled and subnormal children, and centres where young immigrants get intensive coaching in English. We're planning some new special schools because we've found that the outlying areas haven't got enough places, and that means long journeys for the youngsters.

I'm one of the council's representatives on a Gas Consultative Council. We deal with complaints from the public and a Gas Board official tells us about their plans. They're already thinking about developing liquid methane gas when the North Sea supply runs out. This consumer council does a good job but it doesn't get enough publicity. I shall ask next time why its address isn't in the telephone directory.

I attend as many constituency party meetings as I can, and keep in close touch with my ward party (the area I represent). They're not slow to tell me what's wrong and ask what the council's doing about it. I don't miss the party's national speakers if I can help it; they keep us in touch with the big issues of politics.

The new Youth Centre is in my ward, built and owned by the council. I've been chairman of the management committee of the youth club for years, when it didn't have its own building. We shall let the old people and other organizations use it too, but it's mainly for young people.

Mrs Green is a widow, well over seventy. I first met her when I was canvassing in an election. She was in tears. Her street of back-to-back houses was due for demolition and she was terrified of moving, and worried stiff about the rent. I promised to contact the council's Housing Manager and he sent somebody to help her. Six months later I went to see her myself in her new ground-floor council flat. She was all smiles and took me straight to the window to see the beautiful view across the valley. She said how good her neighbours were (some of them from the old street). Her rent was covered by supplementary benefit. For the first time in her life she had a proper kitchen and a bathroom. I shall pop in to see her on the Saturday afternoon.

On Sundays I get down to two or three hours' reading—correspondence and masses of documents from the Civic Hall. It's a very full life and I couldn't manage it without my wife's support. There's no money in being a councillor, except for a few rare crooks. My main work is helping to make this district a better place for our people to live in. There's great satisfaction in that.'

What it takes to be a councillor

Local councillors are not a typical cross-section of the adult population. Surveys done in the 1960s for the Maud (Management) Committee revealed some interesting facts about them.

Age—councillors are older than the national average.
Sex—considerably less than half are women.
Occupation—about one-fifth are retired. More than average are employers, managers, farmers and professional workers. Less than average are skilled and unskilled manual workers.
Education—better than average, especially among younger councillors.

Mobility—more than average were born or have lived a long time in the area they represent.

In some districts local elections are not contested because only one candidate comes forward. In all districts people who would make good councillors quite often turn the idea down. Why?

The commonest reason is lack of time. A wage or salary earner may well think, 'I haven't got enough spare time to attend council and committee meetings, deal with hundreds of people who will bring problems to my door or ring me up, and read piles of documents'.

The wage earner has a legal right to reasonable time off from his employer for council duties. But he may injure his chances of promotion. That could mean a sacrifice for his family as well as himself. (One councillor resigned because his wife said she would leave him if he stayed on the council.) For many women council work is out of the question, unless they are housewives whose children have grown up.

In spite of the difficulties there were more young men and women among the councillors elected in 1973 than previously. The attendance allowances introduced in 1974 made it less likely that councillors would suffer financially, though they pay income tax on the allowances. We probably get a better set of councillors than one might expect.

The Maud (Management) Report, 1967, suggested three requirements for councillors:

a. The capacity to understand sympathetically the problems and points of view of constituents and to convey them to the authority, and at the same time to interpret and explain the authority's policies and actions to those whom they represent.
b. The capacity to understand technical, economic and sociological problems which are likely to increase in complexity.
c. The ability to innovate, to manage, and direct, the personality to lead and guide public opinion and other members; and a capacity to accept responsibilities for the policies of the authority.

If you think that no councillor could be as perfect as that, can you work out a less ambitious list of desirable qualities?

Council staff

Over two million people are employed by local councils. Broadly speaking they fall into four main groups.

Chief Executives and Chief Officers, who manage departments and advise the council.

Administrative, professional and technical staff—librarians, engineers, teachers, surveyors, public health inspectors, social workers, architects, lawyers, weights and measures inspectors, accountants, careers officers.

39

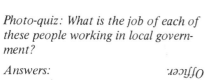

Photo-quiz: What is the job of each of these people working in local government?

Answers:
1. Horticultural Officer; 2. Architectural model-maker; 3. School meals supervisor; 4. Air Traffic Control Officer, Municipal Airport; 5. Senior Assistant Analyst; 6. Scenes of Crime Officer.

Clerical staff—employed in all departments as clerks, secretaries, typists, telephonists, office machine operators.

Manual workers—skilled craftsmen (joiners, plumbers, electricians, bricklayers and so on), road workers, dustmen, canteen assistants, caretakers, cleaners.

The list is by no means complete; can you think of any others? If you have already collected information about council services, you may be able to write a report on the work of at least one kind of employee. Careers booklets about local government are a useful source of information.

Portrait of a Chief Executive

'Mr Gordon Moore lives life at a hot pace. He begins work at 8.30 a.m. and usually he's busy with his civic duties until late at night. Often he's on duty on Saturdays and Sundays.

He landed the plum job of Chief Executive of the Bradford Metropolitan District after sixteen years' work as a solicitor, and later Town Clerk, with five local authorities: Cambridgeshire, Worcester, Bath, Croydon and Bradford.

He says that a Chief Executive is quite a different kind of animal from a Town Clerk. Chief Executives must be able to initiate all sorts of radical and revolutionary ideas and be the instrument by which the new authorities are going to promote their images.

Mr Moore is married and has three children. He is a sidesman at St Peter's Church. Because he has a tidy mind he can't bear to see an untidy garden—so he gardens. He's a lover of railways, music and sport, with a special interest in Yorkshire cricket.

He has resolved not to be connected with any clubs or societies because he believes that in public life he must be seen to be fair and unbiased. Yet he tries to meet as many people as possible. And he talks as if he's hell-bent on blowing cobwebs out of local government.'*

Chief Officers

Local councils give their Chief Officers different titles and the duties vary from place to place. When a new Chief Offficer is appointed the council looks for skill in managing a department, professional qualifications (as a lawyer, teacher, engineer, social worker, accountant and so on) and considerable experience in local government.

A Chief Education Officer usually starts his career as a teacher, moves to administrative work in an Education Department and gradually works his way to the top. A Chief Engineer may get experience with a private firm before he moves to local government, or spend his whole career as a council employee.

The chart on page 42 shows the titles and main responsibilities of some of the Chief Officers in a particular metropolitan district. You

*Shortened version of an article in the Bradford *Telegraph and Argus,* 2 November 1973.

could make a similar but more complete chart for your own councils. Ask the information office or a local councillor for details.

**Responsibilities of Chief Officers
in a Metropolitan District**

Title	Responsibilities
Chief Executive	Council's principal adviser, general manager and co-ordinator
Director of Administration	Secretarial, legal, management and supply services
Director of Develop-ment Services	Highways, housing, markets, planning, public health, refuse collection
Director of Educational Services	Education, libraries, art galleries and museums, baths, theatres, leisure activities (except parks)
Director of Social Services	'Welfare' activities—services for elderly and handicapped, care of children, families in need.
Director of Finance	All financial services, including control of computer.

This council also has a Chief Personnel Officer, responsible for recruitment and training of staff, and a Chief Public Relations Officer. Both officers co-operate with all departments.

Chapter 7
Local government finance

Jack Smith would get a shock if he received an annual bill for Elizabeth's education from the local council. But he helps to pay for it, and for the other local services, through taxes and rates.

Nearly £20 million will be spent on local government services in England and Wales in 1980-81. The amount has increased steadily in your lifetime. Why?

☐ People and governments have demanded better services.

☐ The population increased steadily up to 1979. Children and pensioners use the expensive education and social services most and contribute least to their cost. The numbers of school children rose from 7.8 millions in 1966 to 9.7 millions in 1976 (England and Wales); people over retiring age from 6.6 millions in 1965 to 7.9 millions in 1976. School-pupil numbers will probably fall to 7 millions or 7.5 millions between 1978 and 1988.

☐ Inflation (rising prices) has caused a fall in the value of the pound. So councils have faced the problem of spending more money to provide the same services as before, or the same money on fewer services, or considerably more money on better services.

Where does the money come from?

Revenue income covers the day-to-day costs of running existing services. The money comes from three main sources—government grants, local rates, other local sources.

Capital income covers the provision of new schools, council houses, and public buildings, which will last a long time. The huge sums for new buildings come mainly from loans.

You can get local figures about revenue income and capital income from your council offices. The *Annual Abstract of Statistics* gives the total figures for all local authorities.

Government Grants

The average council gets more that half its income from central government grants (60 per cent in 1980-81). This money is raised by national taxes such as income tax and VAT.

Every year the Government fixes a total amount for grants, after discussions with representative councillors from all over the country. There is a large Rate Support Grant to each council, and much smaller 'specific grants' for certain services such as clean air schemes. In addition, the Government pays housing subsidies, which are not tied down to a total figure.

The Rate Support Grant varies from year to year. It is worked out for each council by a complicated formula, which attempts to even out the differences between rich and poor areas. At present it is based on three 'elements'.

The needs element gives extra money to districts with a high proportion of children under sixteen and people over sixty-five, and to crowded cities.

The resources element compensates councils whose income from rates is below the national standard.

The domestic element compensates all councils for charging lower rates to householders than to industrial and commercial firms.

The councils always ask for bigger grants and criticize the way they are shared out. The Government sometimes alters the formula but keeps the last word about the total figure.

In line with its policy of reducing public expenditure, the Government is to introduce a new system for the rate support grant for 1981-82. A single 'block' grant will take the place of the needs and resources elements in the existing grants and limits will be imposed on capital expenditure. The details are complicated but it is clearly the Government's intention to penalize those councils which are deemed to be 'big spenders'.

Rates

Rates are a local tax on property—houses, factories, offices, shops and so on. They are levied and collected by district councils. They include amounts which are handed over to county councils and parish/community councils, who 'precept' (demand) a proportion to pay for their services. The rate demand note shows how much goes to each council.

Valuation

All property is valued by Valuation Officers, who are employed by the Government's Inland Revenue Department. 'Rateable value' is supposed to be based on the rent at which the property could reasonably be let on the open market. In fact it is nearly always lower.

There are considerable differences between northern and southern counties. For example, a householder moved from a small two-bedroomed house near London (RV £234) to a similar house in Yorkshire (RV £94).

Fixing the rates.

If the district council fixes the general rate at 50p in the pound, it means that 50p is payable for each £1 of rateable value.

First, the council's Finance Department prepares estimates of how much money will be needed in the next financial year. Each council committee discusses its own estimates. The central Policy or Management Committee looks at the whole financial picture and often asks the committees to cut down their spending.

The rate in the pound is worked out by dividing the total estimated expenditure by total rateable value, allowing for income from government grants and other sources. Finally the full council decides next year's rate after heated debates.

44

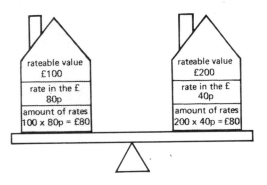

What is the rateable value of your home, and what is the rate in the pound in your district?

Paying the rates.

They can be paid annually, quarterly, or in ten monthly instalments. Council tenants (like Jack Smith) and private tenants often pay weekly, along with their rents. Poorer householders can apply for a rate rebate, which depends on their income and number of dependants.

Other local sources of revenue

Councils vary a great deal in the amounts they raise from other sources—mainly rents and charges for services.

Most service charges are well below the real cost; for example, entrance fees for swimming baths and tennis courts. When you buy a school dinner you are paying for the food, but not for the full cost of preparing and serving it. However, some councils are making changes. What is the position in your area?

County councils charge football clubs the full cost of a police squad at matches. Trading services, such as markets, sometimes show a surplus which helps to reduce the rates. But they may be subsidized, like bus services in some areas, to keep the fares down.

What are the 'other sources' in your district?

How do councils spend the money?

The table on page 46 shows how a metropolitan district council, with a population of 462 000 spent its revenue of £64 millions in 1974-5. How much was that per head? Is the amount likely to have increased or decreased since then?

You can find out how your councils spend the money by borrowing a rate bill. Recent national figures are given in Whitaker's Almanac.

Education is always the most expensive item. In every council department a high proportion of the money is spent on staff salaries and wages, which are fixed by national agreements. That is one reason why councils do not have a lot of choice in deciding how to spend the money.

The rate bill figures show only part of the story. The cost of social security (benefits and pensions) is borne by central govern-

45

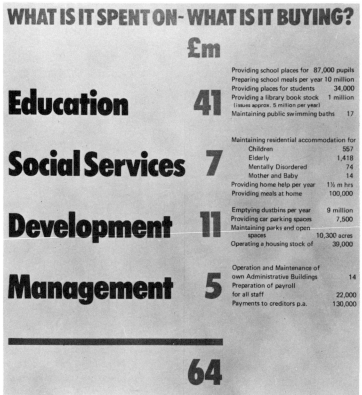

WHAT IS IT SPENT ON - WHAT IS IT BUYING?

£m

Education	**41**	Providing school places for 87,000 pupils Preparing school meals per year 10 million Providing places for students 34,000 Providing a library book stock 1 million (issues approx. 5 million per year) Maintaining public swimming baths 17
Social Services	**7**	Maintaining residential accommodation for Children 557 Elderly 1,418 Mentally Disordered 74 Mother and Baby 14 Providing home help per year 1½ m hrs Providing meals at home 100,000
Development	**11**	Emptying dustbins per year 9 million Providing car parking spaces 7,500 Maintaining parks and open spaces 10,300 acres Operating a housing stock of 39,000
Management	**5**	Operation and Maintenance of own Administrative Buildings 14 Preparation of payroll for all staff 22,000 Payments to creditors p.a. 130,000

64

A year's expenditure by a Metropolitan District Council

Councils can borrow money by advertising in newspapers

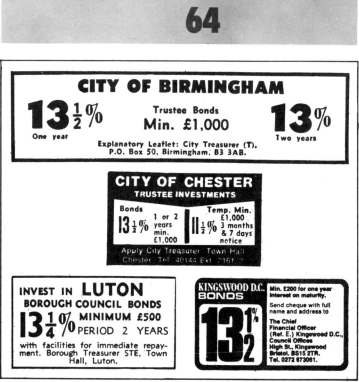

ment, not by local councils. Similarly, the county councils' spending on roads does not include government spending on motorways.

The capital account

Councils borrow most of the money they need for new building schemes. If they tried to pay these huge bills out of annual revenue the rates would fly through the roof, and so would the ratepayers.

Councils have to get 'loan sanction' (Government permission) to borrow money. Each plan for new schools, council houses, and social service buildings usually has to be approved separately, causing delays. But the system is gradually becoming more flexible.

Some councils build up a Capital Fund of their own, putting into it so much money each year from revenue. This fund pays for minor works and extensions but not for the big schemes.

Where do the loans come from? Partly from the Government's National Loans Fund, partly by inviting people and organizations to lend money at a fixed rate of interest for a given period. Other loans are raised for the councils by financial firms in the City of London, or by borrowing abroad.

Every loan has to be paid back with interest, and the annual instalments are paid out of the Revenue Account. (This is rather like a man who pays monthly hire purchase instalments out of his wage.) Housing loans are normally paid off in sixty years; about eighty per cent of a council house weekly rent is spent on repaying the loan.

The annual audit

All council accounts are checked every year by the District Auditor (a civil servant) or by a professionally qualified accountant from outside. Audited accounts are open to public inspection at the council offices.

The Auditor must report any expenditure which is not authorized by Act of Parliament. This is when a councillor who has voted for it can be 'surcharged'. So can a council officer who let it go through. What can you find out about the case of the Clay Cross councillors who refused to obey the Housing Finance Act, 1972, which told councils to raise rents?

A new local finance system?

Councillors often say, 'The Government tells us to provide better services and at the same time tells us to economize. They don't give us enough in grants and we can't raise the rates much more.'

People have grumbled that rates are unfair for many years. The big increases in 1974 sparked off loud demands for a better system.

Defenders of rating say, 'It is an easy tax to collect and difficult to dodge. Once you know the total rateable value of a district it is easy to work out how much a 1p. rate will bring in. It gives a council some independence from central government, because each council decides its own rate in the pound. The poorest householders can get rebates.'

47

Rates doubled in two areas

Anger at rates worries MPs

Councillors receive rate protest

Scrap the present unfair rating system, says MP

Move to head off rates protest

Rating system inquiry

ACTION ON RATE PROTEST URGED

Call for revised rating system

Opponents of rating reply, 'A tax on property is unfair to householders because it bears no relation to their ability to pay. A family with several young children needs a large house, which means high rates. Rateable values stay the same for years on end; when prices are rising rates are bound to go up each year, even if services stay the same. Rates bring in the least money in the poorest areas, where council services are most needed. And rating valuation mystifies people, who can see no sense in the variations.'

If rates were abolished what would replace them? Perhaps bigger government grants to cover the entire cost of expensive items? Councillors want to keep some form of local taxation under their control. Suggestions include a local income tax (as in Norway), local car licence and petrol taxes, local sales tax (as in Canada). Another idea is that Parliament should allow councils to raise more money by trading enterprises—perhaps a chain of filling stations.

Would you agree to higher charges for existing services, for example, paying more for school meals or a swim at the local baths? You will certainly hear a lot more about local government finance.

Chapter 8
Local councils, government and the public

'Why doesn't the council do this, that or the other?' Sometimes the answer is that the Government will not let them do it, or that judges in the law courts would punish them for breaking the law. Or councillors may fear public hostility and losing their seats at the next local election.

Central government control

Local councils are not only bound by Acts of Parliament. Government Ministers and their departments keep a close watch on the way councils carry out the Acts.

An ex-Minister explained it like this. 'The Government lays down essential principles of policy, local councils decide the manner

Local Government Services		*Government Department primarily responsible*
Baths	Parking	Department of Environment
Building regulations	Parks and open spaces	
Cemeteries and crematoria	Planning	
Clean air	Public relations	
Coast protection	Rating	
Conservation areas	Refuse collection	
Country parks	Refuse disposal	
Derelict land clearance	Rights of way	
Entertainments	Road safety	
Highways	Sewers (local)	
Housing	Street cleansing	
Land purchase	Town development	
Lighting: highway and footway	Transport planning	
Litter	Transport undertakings	
Loans for house purchase	Wash-houses	
Art galleries	Playgrounds and playing fields	Department of Education and Science
Education	Youth Employment	
Libraries	Youth services	
Museums		
Community Homes	Shop Acts	Home Office
Fire Service	Weights and Measures	
Police		
Social Services		Department of Health and Social Security
Airports		Department of Industry
Consumer protection		Department of Trade
Allotments	Land drainage	Ministry of Agriculture, Fisheries and Food
Animals (diseases)	Markets	
Food and drugs	Restaurants (civic)	
	Smallholdings	

Responsibility is sometimes transferred to another government department and you should watch out for changes.

in which they are to be carried out. If a council falls down on a job, such as housing, then the Government has a moral right to step in.' Some of the councillors who were listening to his speech muttered, 'Yes, but government departments boss us around about details as well as principles'.

Some of the ways in which the Government exercises control have already been mentioned. Financial control is the strongest weapon, because councils rely heavily on government grants and permission to borrow money. A Minister has the last word in appeals against their planning decisions, and about agency agreements between councils. Bye-laws need a Minister's consent before they are valid.

If a council is dragging its feet, or even refusing to carry out an Act, the Government can order it to complete the job in a certain time. What happens if the council ignores the order? Then a Minister has power to appoint an official to take over the function, or even suspend the council.

Many Acts of Parliament give Ministers power to draw up detailed regulations, which are just as binding as the original Act. Government departments also send advisory circulars to councils, and demand regular reports and statistical returns.

Her Majesty's Inspectors (HMIs) visit schools and colleges and send reports to the Secretary of State for Education, and a copy to the local Education Department. (Has your school been inspected recently?) Police and fire services are regularly visited by inspectors from the Home Office. Inspectors' reports are not made public, but one hears that harsh words are said behind closed doors if council services are below standard.

It adds up to a great deal of Government control, more than in other democratic countries such as Sweden. Councillors strongly resent the fact that local priorities are sometimes decided in London. For example, a county council submitted plans for a new assessment centre (to sort out children in care) and for a new children's home. The Ministry approved the home and turned down the assessment centre, which the council considered much more urgent. 'Instead of local government, all we are getting is local administration of a national service', said an angry Director of Social Services.

On the other hand, local government officers sometimes complain privately that the Government allows their council to get away with a very inferior service. Who is right?

Judicial control by the law courts

Local councils, like individuals, have to obey the ordinary laws of the land, as well as the Acts which specially concern them.

Any citizen can take a council to court and sue it for damages in certain circumstances. You may have heard about parents who sued a local education authority for negligence, because their child had been badly injured in a school gymnasium.

Or suppose that a council's compulsory purchase order has been backed by the Minister after a local public inquiry. That isn't always the end of it. An aggrieved individual, whose house or shop is going to be knocked down, can then appeal to the law courts. The judges look closely for any legal slip-up in the way the council or the Minister has applied the laws about planning.

Councils can take legal action against individuals. If you refuse to pay your rates you may find yourself in court and forced to pay up. A council employee who steals council money or equipment can be prosecuted like any other thief.

Only a lawyer can explain the complications of judicial control. But watch the newspapers for reports of court cases where councils are involved.

Councils and the public

Why do most people show little interest in local government? Is it apathy, lack of information and understanding, or something deeper?

A recent survey showed that young people generally were very ill-informed about politics and not least about local government. Some thought that local councils could change Acts of Partliament when, of course, they are rigidly controlled by them. (R. Stradling, *The Political Awareness of the School Leaver*, Hansard Society, 1977).

As we saw in Chapter 4, turnout for local elections is low in this country. In Sweden, for example, about 80 per cent are likely to vote in local elections and in West Germany about 70 per cent. What steps should be taken to ensure that people are better informed? Should councils give more publicity to what they do?

In recent years some of our councils have set up Information Offices, with professional Public Relations Officers, to inform the public and press about council services and plans. It may be too early for them to have had much effect on voting figures.

Local newspapers report council meetings and print readers' letters, more often complaining about council services than handing out bouquets. At least one editor gets his staff to ring up the council committee Chairman or Chief Officer concerned, and publishes his explanation or apology below the letter. How much coverage does your local newspaper give to council affairs?

The BBC and television companies seem to ignore local councils, apart from giving local election results and news about scandals. 'If it isn't on TV it can't be important.' Is that what people think? Local radio stations invite councillors to their studios and publicize local controversies. Do you ever listen to them?

The public have a legal right to attend council meetings and committees, but the public gallery is rarely full. Some councils organize public meetings, where there is an opportunity for councillors and officials to be questioned and for people to air their views. They attract lively audiences when a new development scheme involves big changes in town centres, or when the rates shoot up. Councillors get a chance to clear up misunderstandings and

Sir — Three children's bus fares to and from school cost 30p per week up to last week.

As from this week, it's 60p.

Why? Because the Transport authority does not recognise half pence.

A small item in the weekly budget, but how typical of our bureaucrats: to penalise those with families for the sake of administrative convenience.

Do their figures make any mention of a 100 per cent increase? Of course not.

A. M. MURPHY,
11 Egremont Crescent,
Woodside.

P.S. They will be walking from now on.

Sir — The kindness and consideration of the staff of the new Shipley swimming pool to our handicapped son when we visited the pool for the first time on June 10, was much appreciated by his father and myself.

Our six-year-old boy is a spastic diplegic (unable to walk) and the staff's concern and encouragement enabled our little boy to enjoy a wonderfully new experience (without any of the apprehension which his father and I felt).

I doubt if the staff can imagine what pleasure it gave us to see our small son actually taking part in an activity which made him the equal of the other "tiddlers."

MARY E. HARRISON.
8 Danum Drive,
Baildon.

Sir — Re the letter headed "Short range of library books" (Telegraph and Argus, May 14), Mrs. Pauline Edwards has stated what I have been longing to say for some time.

While I live in Bradford, I am a frequent user of Leeds Central Library due to this insufficiency.

For example, under the heading "Biography" in Bradford, there appear at the most to be a meagre 50 books available, whereas at Leeds under this same heading one finds row upon row of books to choose from (possibly 1,000).

Also in Bradford some of the books handed out are absolutely filthy — ready for the dustbin — but, of course, to throw them away would mean more empty shelves!

Mrs. MARGARET
AINSCOUGH,
17 Woodhall Place,
Bradford 3.

[Bradford's Chief Librarian, Mr. W. Davies, states: Mrs. Ainscough's letter shows a misunderstanding of the arrangement of Bradford Central Library into subject departments, which means that biographies are related to subject area and are on the appropriate floor. For example, there were, this week, 674 biographies on persons associated with music on the shelves in that department, 361 in art, 120 in commerce, science and technology and in the field of social sciences, which includes local studies, 1,053; whereas in the popular library on the ground floor there were only 80. This gives a total available for loan of 2,288. I do urge readers who cannot find what they want to inquire of the staff. I am perturbed at the allegation that some of the books handed out are "absolutely filthy." I would be pleased if Mrs Ainscough would arrange to call and show me examples of what she means.]

Supermarket trolleys litter an estate

Sir—Re the recent letters concerning rubbish dumped at Buttershaw, we have much the same problems on Canterbury.

At present the field behind my house is used as an unofficial tip. Our view is decorated by two part motor bikes and a burnt out settee. Bins are emptied there if the dust-bin men are late coming round.

That's not the only problem, though. Not a week goes by without someone or something upturning dustbins all over the gardens.

To be fair the council have erected fine big gates at our passage tops. There's no fencing round the gardens, but the gates are lovely.

Also, we have a road hazard all around this estate of supermarket trolleys, either whole ones or in pieces, littering the roads and pavements—a danger to car drivers and pedestrinans alike.

Mrs. B. ANDERSON,
70 Dawnay Road,
Bradford 5.

Industrial estate plan for Otley under fire at protest meeting

Proposals for a 34 acre industrial estate in south-east Otley came under fire at a protest rally.

It was claimed that the scheme was unnecessary, that it was too big, and that it would destroy the balance of Otley as a rural market town.

The meeting, at Otley Civic Centre attended by 250 people followed the presentation of a 3,000 signature petition to Otley Council which is to consider its attitude to the plan next week. Not one of the councillors among the nine speakers at the protest meeting came down in favour of the plan.

Some of the speakers saw no need for any more land for industry in the town saying that unemployment was low and there was already a labour problem. Others said provision must be made for possible future needs but this was not the right site and was too big.

County Coun. Mrs. Eve Fowler told the meeting it was ridiculous to talk of another 34 acres for industry in a town the size of Otley. "It is inviting disaster," she said. "Don't have it. Keep on fighting."

Mr. Nicholas Horton-Fawkes, of Farnley Hall, said they were often urged in planning matters to leave it to the experts but in this case he challenged the experts and saw cause for hope that ordinary people could take a wider and more humanistic view of the quality of life than did the planners.

More than needed

A teacher, Mrs. Anna Oddy, said three new schools were planned in the area and the proposed estate would rob the children of the rural surroundings in which they should develop.

Coun. G. Kirkland, chairman of the council, said the proposed site was double what would be required for a relocation of town centre industries.

A protest rally in a small town

false rumours. But is the audience typical of public opinion, or just a grumbling minority?

Pressure groups, such as Civic Societies and Residents' Associations, often organize their own public meetings and send petitions or delegations to the councils. Local protest groups spring up almost overnight when homes and schools are threatened by plans for urban motorways. The right to form such groups is a valuable democratic safeguard against authority, whether they win, lose or achieve a compromise. And they are not always right. What do people get worked up about in your area?

Every citizen has the right to approach councillors if he has a grievance about the way local services affect him. What happens if the councillor takes up a genuine grouse about a local department and gets nothing done? He can pass the complaint on to a Local Commissioner (popularly known as an Ombudsman) for a thorough investigation of the department concerned. Local Ombudsmen were first appointed in 1974. Since that time the Local Commissioners have drawn attention to a number of cases of *maladministration* by local councils. The authority of these officials is moral not legal. Most councils have done their best to remedy the defects found but if they are stubborn there is no legal power to force them to comply. Is this something that should be changed?

53

Chapter 9
Regional authorities and public corporations

Some important services are run neither by local councils nor by government departments. Parliament has gradually set up a varied collection of regional authorities and public corporations to deal with them.

Since 1945 several services have been taken away from local councils. Governments said that the councils varied too much, or their areas were too small, or they were not capable of running services which needed to be of the same quality all over the country.

☐ Social security (1946 and 1948 Acts); trunk roads and motorways (1946) were transferred to government departments, to be run by civil servants.

☐ Health services (1946 and 1973), water and sewerage (1973) were transferred to special regional authorities.

☐ Electricity (1947) and Gas (1948) were transferred to new public corporations, to be run on a commercial basis.

Most of the members of regional authorities and all the heads of public corporations are appointed by Ministers, not elected by the people.

The idea of 'regions' has grown, especially since we joined the European Economic Community in January 1973. But what is a region? At present there are no generally agreed boundaries. Each regional authority and public corporation makes its own map.

The National Health Service

The National Health Service was reorganized on 1 April 1974, at the same time as the local councils (see chart on facing page). The Chairmen are paid; the other members are part-time and unpaid.

However, the structure then introduced is generally agreed to have been unwieldy and a further reorganization is being planned. The Regional Health Authorities will be retained but the Area Health Authorities will be discontinued. New District Health Authorities will be appointed which will have responsibility for administering the services in their district, including planning provision of primary care and other community health services, as well as hospital services.

The total expenditure on health and personal social services planned for 1980-81 was over £9000 millions. The money for this comes mainly from taxes but a proportion comes from National Insurance contributions and charges for dental treatment, spectacles and so on. Capital spending on new hospitals and Health Centres is covered by government loans.

Family practitioner services include family doctors, dentists, opticians and pharmacists, who make contracts with Area Health Authorities. The average family doctor has a list of 2500 NHS patients. Does your doctor work in a group partnership with its own surgery, or in a Health Centre owned by the Area Health Authority?

Hospitals Nearly all hospitals are owned by AHAs and treatment is free

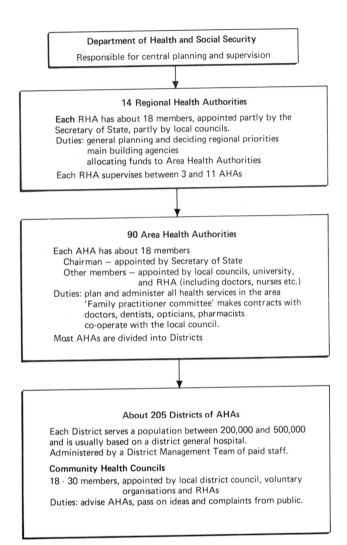

Department of Health and Social Security

Responsible for central planning and supervision

14 Regional Health Authorities

Each RHA has about 18 members, appointed partly by the
Secretary of State, partly by local councils.
Duties: general planning and deciding regional priorities
        main building agencies
        allocating funds to Area Health Authorities
Each RHA supervises between 3 and 11 AHAs

90 Area Health Authorities

Each AHA has about 18 members
    Chairman — appointed by Secretary of State
    Other members — appointed by local councils, university,
               and RHA (including doctors, nurses etc.)
Duties: plan and administer all health services in the area
    'Family practitioner committee' makes contracts with
        doctors, dentists, opticians, pharmacists
    co-operate with the local council.
Most AHAs are divided into Districts

About 205 Districts of AHAs

Each District serves a population between 200,000 and 500,000
and is usually based on a district general hospital.
Administered by a District Management Team of paid staff.

Community Health Councils
18 - 30 members, appointed by local district council, voluntary
           organisations and RHAs
Duties: advise AHAs, pass on ideas and complaints from public.

How the National Health Service is organized. (But note changes from 1983. See page 54.)

when you need it. (Some people join medical insurance schemes, which pay for private treatment.) How many hospitals are there in your area and of what types?

Personal services include clinics for mothers and young children, school health services, home nurses and midwives, health visitors, vaccination and immunization, care and after-care (for example, for people who have had tuberculosis). Has your family used any of these services?

Our National Health Service is probably the best in the world, but it is not perfect and gets plenty of criticism.

Have we got our priorities wrong? We spend much more on hospitals than on family doctors, much more on drugs and medicines than on health education and preventing disease. If there were more Health Centres fewer people would have to go to hospitals for X-rays

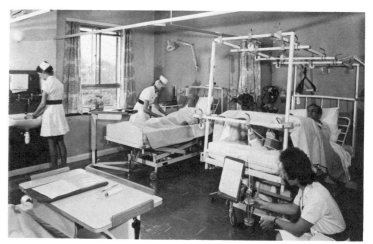

Part of a hospital ward at Bromley Accident and Emergency Centre

Visiting the clinic

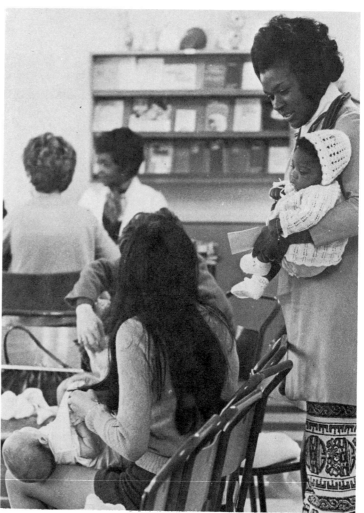

and tests.

Hospitals complain about staff shortages of doctors and nurses; physiotherapists, radiographers, occupational therapists, speech therapists; ambulance men; porters, cleaners and kitchen staff. The staff say that shortages would disappear if they were better paid.

There are political arguments about whether we should keep or abolish 'pay beds' for private patients in National Health Service hospitals; take drug manufacturing firms into public ownership; set up an Occupational Health Service to treat people at work.

Do patients with real or imaginary grievances get a fair deal? The Community Health Councils pass on complaints to the Area Health Authorities. There are two Health Service Commissioners (Ombudsmen) with limited powers to investigate. Patients can go to the civil law courts, but that is an expensive procedure. Perhaps there would be fewer imaginary grievances if doctors had more time to explain things.

Can you suggest any ways in which the health services might be improved?

Water and sewerage

Demand for water by householders and industries will probably double by the year 2001, and some areas are already short of water in dry weather.

Before 1 April 1974, about 1600 public bodies (including local councils) and private firms were responsible for water, sewerage and rivers. They all lost their water and sewage works by the Water Act, 1973, which transferred these services to ten new Regional Water Authorities and a National Water Council to co-ordinate their work. County and district councils nominate more than half the RWA members; the others are appointed by the Government. District Councils can provide sewers as agents of the Regional Water Authorities.

There are plans to build new reservoirs, enlarge existing ones, and link up the separate water systems by means of rivers, new artificial aqueducts and underground pumping. It will cost a great deal of money; water rates already went up sharply in 1974.

You may have read about the terrible cholera and typhoid epidemics in the nineteenth century. They were caused by germs which were carried by sewage-polluted drinking water. Sanitary and water engineers claim that we owe as much to them as to doctors.

When the Regional Water Authorities took over, they found that in some areas raw, untreated sewage was still pumped into river estuaries and the sea, instead of being filtered at sewage works.

Many rivers and canals are polluted by industrial waste and poisonous chemicals, which make them an eyesore and a menace to health. The former River Authorities had begun to get tough with polluters. In 1960 no fish, except eels, could survive in the filthy tidal Thames. By 1974 there were sixty-six different species of fish swimming around. But human swimmers are still advised to keep their mouths shut if they bathe in our inland waterways.

A badly polluted river

Regional economic planning councils

Since 1921 it has been obvious that some regions suffer more than others from unemployment, declining industries, and a lower standard of living. In 1965 the Government set up ten Regional Economic Planning Councils, as part of its plans for encouraging economic growth.

They were told to 'study and advise on the needs and potentialities of their regions and on the development of long-term planning strategy'. Studies were to include the social services, as well as economic and transport problems. A job is not much use to a man if he has no house to live in and no schools for his children.

Unlike the health and water authorities, these councils were given no executive powers; they could only 'study and advise'. They have had the help of Regional Planning Boards, whose members are senior civil servants in the regional offices of government departments.

All ten councils have issued detailed reports about the decline of old industries and the rise of new ones, with forecasts of population and employment trends. They have advised new patterns of industrial development, new ways in which the Government can help hard-hit regions, improvements in roads, airports and bridges.

It sounds impressive and some of their advice has been accepted. But they exist uncomfortably between central government and local councils—which grimly hang on to their own planning and transport powers.

58

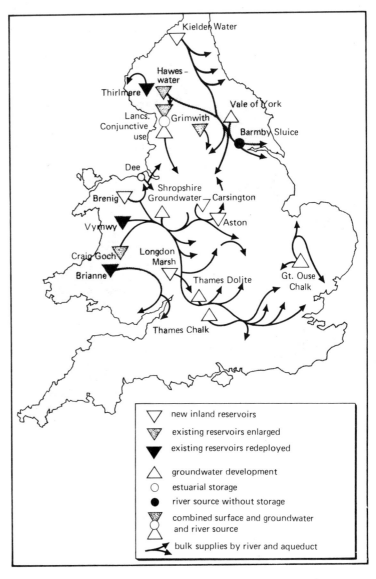

Kielder Water

Hawes-
water

Thirlmere

Vale of York

Lancs.
Conjunctive
use

Grimwith

Barmby Sluice

Dee

Brenig

Shropshire
Groundwater

Carsington

Aston

Vyrnwy

Craig Goch

Longdon
Marsh

Gt. Ouse
Chalk

Brianne

Thames Dolite

Thames Chalk

new inland reservoirs

existing reservoirs enlarged

existing reservoirs redeployed

groundwater development

estuarial storage

river source without storage

combined surface and groundwater
and river source

bulk supplies by river and aqueduct

The water resources of England and Wales (Source: 'Water Resources in England and Wales', 1974, HMSO)

(N.B. Tinted areas, unmarked by arrows, are self-sufficient)

Public corporations

Have you heard of the Arts Council, National Parks Commission, Countryside Commission, British Council, BBC? These are just a few of the 200 or so special bodies which governments have appointed and given a varying amount of freedom and money to get on with their tasks.

In the late 1940s some of the basic industries were nationalized— taken over from privately-owned companies and (in the case of electricity and gas) from some of the local councils: coal mines, railways, certain bus services and road haulage, the major airlines, atomic energy, electricity, gas, and the largest steel works. They are all run by public corporations; so is the Post Office, which used to be a government department. The Post Office is now divided into *two* corporations, one for postal and 'giro' services and the other for telecommunications. (The Government also intends to end the Post Office's long-standing monopoly in postal and telecommunication services. Do you think this is a good move or a bad one?)

The National Coal Board is a good example of how a public corporation works. An Act of Parliament defines its responsibilities —to produce as much coal as the country needs, as economically as possible. The Minister responsible for Energy appoints the Board's members and lays down general policy. For example, during the 1960s the NCB was told to close a lot of pits and produce less coal because the demand for it was declining. Then the price of oil rose steeply in 1973 and the Board was instructed to open up new pits and produce more coal. In June 1981 it was announced that the Government was to provide a grant of £550 millions to the N.C.B. to finance 'uneconomic' pits, subsidize coal and coke prices, and generally assist in offsetting working losses. (Is the Government wise to interfere in this way?)

All the industrial public corporations are free to manage their day-to-day affairs. They rely on the Government for investment capital to modernize the railways, build new power stations and gas pipe-lines, new steel works and so on. With the exception of coal, they are organized on a regional basis; for example, there are twelve area Electricity Boards, which fix slightly different prices for customers.

Consultative or Consumer Councils which were intended to represent customers' interests and to investigate their complaints were set up for the coal, gas, electricity and transport undertakings, and for the Post Office. But there are doubts about how effective these bodies have proved to be. Can you identify these bodies and find out where and how to make representations to them?

What next?

Does it matter whether services are run by local councils, regional authorities, public corporations or government departments? Most people never give it a thought, provided the services are efficient.

A critical minority thinks that organization does matter, and that our present system is an unsatisfactory and undemocratic hotch-potch. Councillors resent the loss of gas, electricity, health services, water and sewerage, to non-elected and remote bodies. 'These members appointed by the Government aren't representative; they don't have to explain what they're doing to the electors, or meet them face to face as we do.'

But some public services do need larger areas than the present local councils. It makes sense to plan water supplies on the geographical basis of watersheds and river estuaries. 'All right', say the critics, 'then let's have elected regional councils, to run regionally-based services, and perhaps take over passenger transport

3

5

2

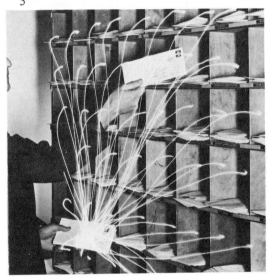

1

4

Photo-quiz: These photographs are all taken from larger pictures of scenes in different nationalized industries: Coal, Steel, Post Office, Railways, and Electricity. Can you guess which is which?

Answers:

1. The Post Office; 2. British Steel Corporation; 3. National Coal Board; 4. British Rail; 5. Central Electricity Generating Board.

20 questions & answers

Q.1. What is Plaid Cymru?

Plaid Cymru is the National Party of Wales—the only political party to represent Wales in parliament.

Plaid Cymru has three aims:-
(i) we seek self government for Wales within the Commonwealth so that the people of Wales shall have freedom to control their own affairs;
(ii) our policies are designed to strengthen the social and economic life of Wales and its language;
(iii) we believe that Wales should take a full part in world affairs as a member of the United Nations Organisation.

Plaid Cymru was founded in 1925. Today it has over 40,000 members throughout Wales, and more and more people share our aims.

In the historic by-election at Carmarthen in 1966, Gwynfor Evans was elected as Plaid Cymru M.P. to speak for the whole of Wales. The tremendous swing to Plaid Cymru was confirmed at Rhondda and Caerffili where mammoth Labour majorities were destroyed. The swing in these elections was larger than in any elections in Britain since the war.

The most exciting part of these elections were the questions people asked at packed meetings: intelligent, penetrating questions about the problems and possibilities of a self-governing Wales.

Those questions are the basis of this pamphlet.

Q.2. Isn't Wales too small for self-government?

The twentieth century is the age of the small nation. There are now 39 nations in the world, smaller than Wales in population, but with complete self-government and full membership of the United Nations Organisation. These include such advanced nations as Iceland, Luxembourg and New Zealand.

At the same time, almost every large country in the world is divided into smaller regions with a substantial measure of self-government, each with its own government, its own parliament, its own laws.

The U.S.A. is a nation of 50 states, more than half of these being smaller in population than Wales. Yet each state has its own constitution and its own laws.

1

THE AIMS AND FUNDAMENTAL OUTLOOK OF THE SCOTTISH NATIONAL PARTY

AIMS:
(a) Self-government for Scotland: that is, the restoration of Scottish National Sovereignty by the establishment of a democratic Scottish Parliament, within the Commonwealth, freely elected by the Scottish people, whose authority will be limited only by such agreements as may be freely entered into by it with other nations or states or international organisations for the purpose of furthering international co-operation and world peace.
(b) The furtherance of all Scottish interests.

The outlook of the Scottish National Party is reflected in the following statements on the fundamentals of society, as first accepted and published by the Party in 1964.

All human beings, no matter how different in gift or achievement, are entitled to equal opportunity and consideration, and society should be developed, and wealth distributed, so as to give everyone the freedom and dignity which is his or her right.

The SNP recognises the need to build towards a true fraternity of all nations, with policies based on the rule of law: freedom of conscience, expression and worship; collective defence; and positive measures to remove the poverty and injustice which threaten the peace of the world.

The SNP recognises that no nation can benefit by isolation and that the needs of world peace and stability depend on nations agreeing among themselves to yield sovereignty in certain respects.

The SNP believes in the progressive development of national, regional and community government and other institutions, towards the greatest possible diffusion of democratic power and responsibility, to reverse the harmful effects of the centralising forces which have been at work in government and industry and finance, controlling Scotland from outside it.

To the SNP, sound and practical policies are those which will ensure that all are decently housed and in good health, and that all have an equal chance of living active and happy lives, and of developing the talents with which they are endowed.

The Scottish National Party will achieve these aims through the democratic support of the Scottish people at the polls. We are a nation. We must act as one so that the rest of the world sees clearly that the Scottish people mean to accept the responsibilities of a nation.

3

Above left: From a Plaid Cymru (The National Party of Wales) leaflet, '20 Questions And Answers'

Above right: From a Scottish National Party leaflet, Scotland's Future, S.N.P. Manifesto, August 1974

as well from the county councils'. That would mean another set of local elections, or perhaps indirect elections—district and county councils might elect the members of new regional councils.

Devolution

Meanwhile there has been a strong growth of *nationalism* in Scotland and Wales. The Scottish National Party and Plaid Cymru want their countries to break away from the United Kingdom and become independent states. They ask at least for their own Parliaments, with powers to pass laws about most things. This nationalist feeling goes beyond a general impatience with remote control from London.

In 1969 the Government appointed a Royal Commission on the Constitution, to study the whole problem of national and regional demands for change. After four years they issued majority and minority reports, because the members of the Commission could not agree among themselves. The majority recommended elected assemblies and governments for Scotland and Wales, but not complete independence. They suggested eight advisory regional councils for England. (Kilbrandon Report, November 1973.)

A few months later the Scottish National Party won seven seats in the general election of February 1974. The three main political parties put forward plans for a new Scottish 'Assembly', with considerable powers to make laws. But the Scottish National Party increased its score to eleven seats in the October 1974 general election. Plaid Cymru won three seats.

After two years of discussion, the Government introduced a Scotland and Wales Bill, to give both countries new elected Assemblies with limited powers (30 November 1976). There were stormy debates in the House of Commons. The Scottish and Welsh Nationalists said that the Bill did not go far enough; most Conservatives and some Labour M.P.s said that it went too far. The Government was defeated on a 'guillotine' motion to cut short the debates (22 February 1977), and eventually had to drop the Bill. They promised to introduce two separate Devolution Bills, with minor changes, in the next session of Parliament.

After a nine-month struggle in Parliament the Scotland Act and the Wales Act became law in July 1978. Both Acts provided for referendums about devolution, to be followed by direct elections for Scottish and Welsh Assemblies if at least 40 per cent of *registered electors* voted 'Yes'. (The normal rule is 50 per cent of actual voters.) The referendums were held on 1 March 1979. In Wales the result was clear — 'No'. In Scotland the 40 per cent target was not reached, although over 50 per cent of the actual voters said 'Yes'.

	Actual voters (%)			Registered electors (%)		
	YES	NO	Turnout	YES	NO	Did not vote
Scotland	51.6	48.3	62.9	32.5	30.4	37.1
Wales	20.3	79.7	58.3	11.8	46.5	41.7

In the light of this result no further Government action has been taken. Both the S.N.P. and Plaid Cymru retain their objectives but the prospect of achieving these, in the short run at least, seems to have dimmed.

Northern Ireland

Northern Ireland is another story and a tragic one of two communities at loggerheads. The Protestant majority want to stay in the United Kingdom; many Catholics, who suffered discrimination over a long period, would prefer to join up with the Republic of Ireland in the south.

Up to 1972 Northern Ireland had its own Parliament which dealt with all domestic matters. After a period of serious disturbances this was dissolved and the province has been ruled directly from Westminister since that time. Attempts to introduce a system of 'power-sharing' failed.

The I.R.A. (Irish Republican Army) continues its campaign of terrorism and Protestant extremists retaliate. The problem so far has defied any satisfactory solution.

Chapter 10
What is central government about?

About 1100 years ago King Alfred the Great *was* the central government. He decided what the laws should be and tried to enforce them. Central government has now become an interwoven set of institutions, especially Parliament, H.M. Government (including the Cabinet) and the Civil Service.

If anybody had asked King Alfred what central government was about, he would probably have replied, 'Keeping law and order inside my kingdom and defending it from its enemies, those evil Danes'. In our highly complex society government is still concerned with law and order and defence, but many other problems have loomed up:

☐ economic and financial problems
☐ industrial relations between employers and employees
☐ social problems, such as housing, education and poverty
☐ foreign affairs—Britain's role in the world.

Which problems are being highlighted by the press and television as you read this book?

Economic and Financial Problems

Economics is the study of how wealth is produced and distributed. To an economist 'wealth' means goods and services—anything from a pen to a bus ride. Money is only a handy way of exchanging goods and services. A pile of banknotes or a credit card would be useless if you were marooned on a desert island; a box of matches would be much more valuable.

During the last fifty years governments have become deeply involved in economic activities. You don't have to be an economist or a politician to realize that rising prices and unemployment affect ordinary families—who are also voters and expect government action.

Rising prices

Margaret Smith is horrified by the way her weekly shopping bill has gone up. Her mother tells them that when she was Elizabeth's age you could buy fish and chips for 3½d. (old pence).

Prices have risen in this country every year since 1935. Economists call it inflation. It is a problem which has baffled governments in nearly every country in the Western world.

What causes rising prices? The simplest explanation is scarcity in relation to demand. If the whole world is shrieking for scarce oil, the producers push up the prices.

Some government taxes increase prices, especially the Value Added Tax which falls on most goods and services. (But governments can also lower or stabilise prices by subsidizing necessities such as milk and bread.)

Why do manufacturers raise the prices of the goods they produce? It may be to make higher profits for their shareholders. But publicly-owned industries sometimes have to raise their prices, too, because their costs have risen. Manufacturers' costs include three main items:

64

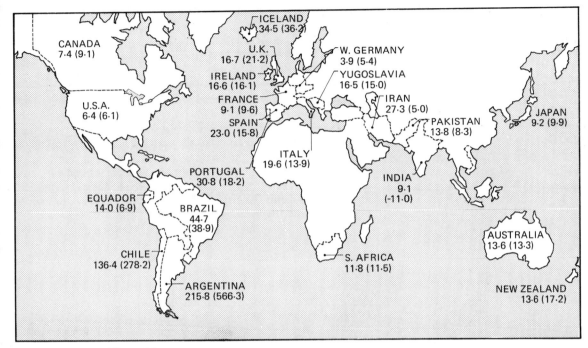

Inflation - the world's problem

The map shows inflation rates at the end of March 1977. The figures in brackets show inflation rates for the previous year, at the end of March 1976. (Source: IMF 'International Financial Statistics')

□ Raw materials, such as iron ore, copper, wood; most of these are imported and if world prices go up the manufacturer, private or public, has to pay them.

□ Overhead costs, such as rent and rates, heating and lighting, maintenance and repairs, insurance.

□ Wages and salaries, which are often the biggest item.

If these costs go up a manufacturer may be able to absorb some of them by using more efficient methods. Firms in the private sector may decide to reduce the shareholders' dividends, which are paid out of profits, or reduce the amount of money set aside for new machinery or buildings. But really bad inflation will force them to raise prices eventually.

And rising incomes

When people find that prices are rising they naturally ask for higher wages. But if Jack Smith gets a five per cent rise at a time when the cost of living is also rising by five per cent, he is no better off. His 'money wage' has gone up but his 'real wage' is the same.

Then a 'vicious spiral' develops—higher money wages → higher production costs → higher prices → higher money wages. What can the Government do about it? Try to control both prices and incomes at the same time, or concentrate on one of them, or just let things rip?

Most wealthy people get all or part of their incomes from

profits/dividends or from rents for the land and property they own. So an 'incomes policy' is not simply about wages and salaries.

The main problem is how to keep incomes of all kinds roughly in line with the total output of goods and services. Printing more paper money does not produce wealth, but it does push prices upwards.

Unemployment

When Jack Smith heard that he might lose his job it worried him much more than the fire on his allotment. Some of his workmates talked about 'sitting-in' and refusing to be sacked.

Mass unemployment was a nightmare during the inter-war years rising to a peak of at least three millions in 1933. After 1945 it looked as if governments had licked the problem, except in regions which depended on declining industries. In the mid-1960s there were shortages of labour, especially of skilled workers. Young people wondered why their fathers still feared the sack.

But the situation of virtually full employment which Britain had during this period (when the Prime Minister, Mr Harold Macmillan, coined the phrase 'You've never had it so good') has now dramatically changed. Unemployment rose steadily throughout the 1970s. In 1969 the total out of work was about 534 000; by 1971 it had reached nearly 1 million, the worst figure for over thirty years. But worse was to come. By March 1980 unemployment had reached the 1½ million mark; by March 1981 it had increased by a further million to 2½ millions, with indications that the total may rise still further.

This means that, in 1981, at least one in ten of the working population was unemployed. Some areas are worse hit than others, with the North of England, Scotland, Wales and Northern Ireland having a higher rate of unemployment than the South of England. In some districts more than 40 per cent were without jobs.

Unemployment creates a number of serious problems for the families of those affected — and not least for young people. What is the nature of these problems and how, if at all, can they be alleviated? What steps have been taken by the Government in an effort to help young people who have no job? When and how is the general situation likely to improve?

What causes unemployment? Old occupations such as riveting disappear. Once flourishing industries decline—in the case of railways because people changed to motor transport. Automation (new machinery which reduces physical and mental labour) has cut out hundreds of thousands of semi-skilled and unskilled jobs.

Over the years new industries have developed and governments have tried to steer them into regions of above-average unemployment. There has been a steady fall in the proportion of workers employed in manufacturing industries and a steady rise in service industries. Mum probably worked in a factory when she left school; her daughter is more likely to work in an office or shop.

The total number of jobs depends to a large extent on whether the economy as a whole is thriving and since the 1970s Britain has been affected by a worsening economic situation that is world-wide.

66

How far can Governments manage and control the economy? In no field of Government action is there more disagreement about what is the sensible thing to do to control or improve a situation, especially when it is going badly. It can certainly release more spending power by lowering taxes, or it can do the opposite of this. By lowering or raising bank interest rates it can make money easier or more difficult for businesses to borrow. There is a whole range of techniques which the Government can use but their use depends on its judgement of the situation and what it hopes to achieve. Even then the outcome of the measures taken is by no means certain.

The British economy is highly dependent on selling goods and services to customers all over the world. If world trade sneezes our industries are apt to catch a severe cold. Which leads to another difficult problem.

Balance of payments

Countries sometimes run into debt because they spend more abroad than they earn. Unlike individuals they cannot dodge the debt by doing a 'moonlight flit'.

Balancing our trading accounts with the rest of the world is a complicated business.

The balance of trade is the difference in value between exports and imports of goods. In most years since the mid-nineteenth century Britain has spent more on importing goods than it has earned by exporting goods.

The balance of payments or 'current account' includes invisible exports and imports as well as goods. British banks, insurance, merchant shipping, airlines and tourist firms sell millions of pounds worth of services to foreigners. British companies and individuals receive interest on their investments abroad. In good years all these invisible exports more than make up for any trade gap in goods.

The capital account covers movements of money for investment into and out of Britain. For example, Ford's Dagenham factory was built with American capital; the Leyland factories in Africa were built with British capital. In addition, many foreigners deposit money with London financial firms, provided interest rates are temptingly high. But they are apt to withdraw this money suddenly if they get the jitters or find a more profitable place.

A shaky economy and a balance of payments deficit together affect the value of the pound in relation to other currencies. If the Government devalues the pound our exports sell more cheaply abroad, but imports cost more. So prices at home get another shove upwards.

If the balance of payments is in the red, governments first dip into their reserves (savings). If the deficit is huge they borrow money from foreign bankers or the International Monetary Fund. At home the Government tries to stimulate exports and cut back imports, to get the future balance right.

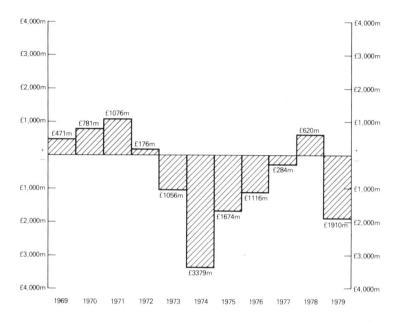

*Britain's balance of payments, current account 1969-79
(Source: Annual Abstract of Statistics, HMSO, 1981)*

Economic growth

Economic growth has come in fits and starts since 1945. The output of goods and services has increased and so have standards of living, but more slowly than in other industrial countries. By 1974 Britain seemed to have dropped into the second division of the economic league, along with Italy and Ireland.

An American economist has blamed lack of capital investment in British industries, to replace ancient machines which ought to have been sent to museums. 'British capitalists prefer to invest abroad, where they will make more money.' He also blamed low productivity—low output per worker. People disagree whether this is due to laziness, lack of efficient machines, poor management, or poor wages.

All industrial countries were hit by steep rises in world prices, and by a scarcity of oil and essential raw materials, in the winter of 1973-4. For a time governments stopped talking about economic growth and wondered if they could keep the existing level of production and living standards.

Scientists have warned us for years that we are an extravagant lot, burning up nature's fuels (oils, coal and gas) and cutting down forests as if they were limitless. Coal has become precious again and the development of North Sea oil and nuclear power has been speeded up.

68

No post-war British government has solved the problem of how to secure economic growth and full employment without running into inflation and balance of payments problems.

Distribution of wealth

Wealth is created by millions of people working together in a huge jig-saw of production. When people ask how the wealth is shared out, and why it is shared out in a particular way, they are really talking about the basis of our economy and society.

this privileged group in the adult population — owns this share of the total personal wealth (shown shaded)

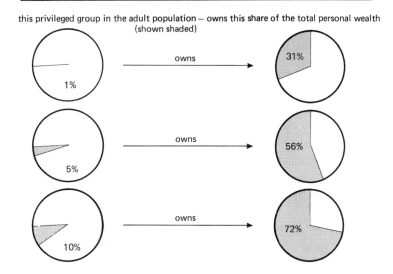

Estimated distribution of personal wealth
(Source: Hansard, 29 March 1973)

Britain has a 'mixed economy'. Well over half our industries are privately owned by over two and a half million shareholders and by large financial organizations such as insurance companies. Less than half our industries are owned by public corporations. In addition, certain firms, such as Rolls Royce, have been wholly or partly nationalized.

In recent years many of the private sector companies have merged into huge groups, such as Imperial Chemical Industries. Some of them are 'conglomerates' and own firms in several industries. The largest and economically most powerful groups are 'multi-nationals' which own factories and so on all over the world.

Is it possible for governments to control these economic giants? They have tried to do so, but with little effect on the distribution of wealth. The lion's share continues to go to the people who own the companies.

Few people imagine that it is possible (or desirable?) to share out wealth equally at so much per head. But we shall go on arguing for a long time about the fairness of distribution and how to achieve it.

Industrial Relations

People feel strongly about wages. 'I've had a long training', says the qualified nurse. 'I deserve more than our cleaners and porters'. (Differentials in the same industry.) 'It isn't right that car manufacturing workers should earn more than miners.' (Relativities between workers in different industries.) Wages are based on several factors, including bargaining power.

Industrial disputes – international comparisons

Average for ten years 1969-78

Country	No. of days
UK	897
Australia	1 242
Belgium	467
Canada	1 929
Denmark	575
Finland	1 143
France	297
West Germany	90
India	1 379
Irish Republic	991
Italy	1 938
Japan	231
Netherlands	75
New Zealand	525
Norway	79
Spain	928
Sweden	42
USA	1 282

(*Source: ACAS, Industrial Relations Handbook, HMSO, 1980, App. 3, P. 300*)

It is often thought that Britain is the most strike-prone country in the world. What does this table show?

Growth of trade union membership, 1900–1978

Year	TU membership as % of workforce
1900	11.7
1910	13.4
1920	34.9
1930	26.4
1940	31.6
1950	44.3
1960	40.5
1970	44.9
1971	45.0
1972	45.8
1973	45.5
1974	46.6
1975	47.9
1976	48.1
1977	49.4
1978	50.3

(*Source: ACAS, Industrial Relations Handbook, HMSO, 1980, App. 4, p. 302*)

Which workers are (a) most likely, (b) least likely, to be members of a trade union? Which are the biggest trade unions?

Trade unions exist to get the best possible wages and conditions for their members. Employers' associations exist to protect the interests of their member firms or public services. Each side of industry has a central body–the Trades Union Congress and the Confederation of British Industry. Governments consult both.

Trade unions and employers' associations have built up a complex system of 'collective bargaining' round the table. Their agreements normally fix wages, hours, holidays and so on, for four-fifths of all employees in Britain.

Sometimes wage negotiations reach deadlock because neither side will budge, or because a government lays down unacceptable conditions. An industrial dispute follows—a ban on overtime, a strike by the union or a lock-out by employers. Should governments intervene or leave them to fight it out, or try to help by setting up arbitration and conciliation machinery to resolve the disputes peacefully?

Both Labour and Conservative governments since 1945 have tried out voluntary and compulsory incomes policies as part of their attempts to control inflation. They have passed different laws about industrial relations and disputes. What is the current situation in these respects?

But industrial relations are not just about wages and working conditions. 'Every citizen should have a voice in the conduct of the business or industry which is carried on by means of his labour, and the satisfaction of knowing that his labour is directed to the well-being of the community.' (Archbishop Temple, 1941.) Do you agree?

Social Problems

Just over a hundred years ago the social services hardly existed. At least half the children never went to school, or only for a year or two. Most people rarely visited a doctor unless they were at death's door. Old age, sickness and unemployment often meant scraping along in abject poverty or the humiliation of entering the work-house. The death-rate, especially of babies, was high.

When social problems arise, the first steps to improve things are usually taken by voluntary societies. This was the case in Britain in the nineteenth century. But a large, complicated industrial society needs new ways of tackling social problems; they become too big for individuals, families and churches to solve alone.

You may have studied the origins of the social services, when governments began to lay the foundations of what we now call the Welfare State. Most of our present social services are based on Acts passed in the 1940s, which put the responsibility for social problems on the whole nation.

Social Security and poverty

By 1946 there was general agreement that benefits and pensions ought to be the same throughout the country. The National Insurance and other Acts established new, comprehensive social security schemes, and gave the job of administering them to government departments and civil servants.

The method of raising money, by weekly national insurance stamps and general taxes, was strongly criticized in the early 1970s. From 6 April 1975 stamp cards for employees were abolished. Earnings-related national insurance contributions are now collected along with income tax.

More important, there are arguments about the extent to which the Government should help people in need and how it should be done. In 1974 there were forty-four separate means tests for different state welfare schemes, including supplementary benefits.

71

But at least forty per cent of the people who are entitled to means-tested benefits never take them up, either because they don't know how to, or because they are too proud to do so. Do you know why some people hate means tests?

The problem of poverty persists, especially among retired people, low wage-earners with families, and unsupported mothers—separated, deserted, divorced, or unmarried.

Unemployment can also cause poverty. A sample survey in June 1973, showed that thirty per cent of unemployed adults were keen to find work but had poor prospects of finding it. At that time most of them were too old, or physically or mentally handicapped. (*See Department of Employment Gazette,* March 1974). When unemployment is very heavy the main reason for poor prospects is likely to be sheer lack of jobs.

Poverty in Britain today

Housing, Education and Health

Some of the issues are outlined in Chapters 2 and 9. In all these services, whether they are run by local councils or by appointed regional authorities, the Government decides the policies which shape them and, to a large extent, the amount of money they get.

Foreign Affairs

In political discussions, domestic matters tend to figure more prominently than foreign affairs. Even in general elections foreign policy issues are likely to be forced into the background. Britain is no longer the important military and economic power that once it was but it has important links with international bodies such as the European Economic Community and the Commonwealth. Britain, like other countries today, cannot turn its back to the rest of the world and the many problems which exist.

Whatever the headlines may say, three problems stand out—the division of the world into rich and poor nations; racial and colour conflicts; local wars and the fear of a nuclear Third World War. In practice all three are mixed up together.

Rich and poor nations

Perhaps you already know something about the problems of poverty and hunger in parts of Africa, Asia and South America. How far should British governments (and other rich relations) help them and in what ways? Some people say, 'Help our own poor at home first',

Poverty in Africa today

or 'Leave it to private investors to provide the capital these countries need for economic development', or 'Leave it to Oxfam and the Red Cross.'

In the early 1970s the British Government paid out about £250 millions a year in direct aid to developing countries. Partly in grants, mainly in loans, and partly in technical assistance—sending doctors, engineers, agricultural scientists and teachers, to help with training and getting things started. By 1977 British Government direct aid had risen to £670 millions a year, mainly in grants and concentrated on the poorest countries.

Governments of poor countries sometimes say bitterly that they wouldn't need any handouts or loans if the people in rich countries were prepared to pay fair prices for their products and labour. 'We want trade, not aid.'

Race and colour

Hatred and exploitation of men whose faces are the 'wrong' colour, or whose noses are the 'wrong' size, are nothing new.

We read about apartheid in South Africa, but the problem of racial discrimination literally comes home in the back streets of Birmingham and Brixton. Some readers of this book are probably immigrants, who can explain why people pull up their roots and move to other countries.

British governments handle the problem gingerly. Parliament passed Acts in 1962, 1968 and 1971 to restrict immigration to people with work permits, and to the close dependants of people already settled here. By 1970 there were about one and a half million permanent settlers.

The Race Relations Acts of 1965, 1968 and 1976 made racial discrimination in housing, employment and the provision of services illegal. Roy Jenkins, as Home Secretary, defined social integration as 'equal opportunity, accompanied by cultural diversity, in an atmosphere of tolerance.' Can you think of a better definition?

War and peace

The world is still a political jungle, where nations arm themselves to the teeth, have little faith in the United Nations Organization, and seek refuge in military alliances, such as the North Atlantic Treaty Organization and the Warsaw Pact.

All British politicians heaved sighs of relief in 1973 when the two big powers, the United States and the Soviet Union, began to thaw out their mutual hostility. There even seemed to be hope of world and European agreements on disarmament, or at least some limitation on the growth of arms.

The European Community

Since 1950 the nations of Western Europe have healed the bitter quarrels which sparked off two World Wars in 1914 and 1939.

Six nations originally formed the European Community (Common Market). After long arguments—go in or stay out?—the United Kingdom entered the Community on 1 January 1973. Stay in or get

74

out? That was settled by the National Referendum on 5 June 1975.

Should the European Community continue as a group of nation states, mainly concerned with economic problems? Or gradually change into a political and economic union, with a European Government and a directly elected Parliament?

National Referendum, 5 June 1975

A majority voted 'Yes' to stay in the European Community.

YES	17,378,581	67.2 per cent
NO	8, 470,073	32.8 per cent
Majority	8,908,508	

	Yes	No
England	68.7%	31.3%
Scotland	58.4%	41.6%
Wales	64.8%	35.2%
N. Ireland	52.1%	47.9%

By 1979 the main British parties wanted changes in the Common Agricultural Policy, to reduce food surpluses and high prices. The United Kingdom was clearly paying more than its fair share into the European Community's Budget. This is a matter which is still fiercely debated both within and without the EEC.

Before 1979 the *European Assembly* (or Parliament) had only 198 members (36 from the United Kingdom), who were all members of their national parliaments and chosen by their colleagues. The first direct elections were held on 7 and 10 June 1979, for 410 members (81 from the United Kingdom). The Liberals, who have been active supporters of EEC membership, did not win a single seat. How do you account for this?

European Assembly Election, 7-10 June 1979

Seats won	Belgium	Denmark	France	West Germany	Ireland	Italy	Luxem-burg	Nether-lands	United Kingdom	Total
Communists		1	19			24				44
Socialists	7	3	21	35	4	13	1	9	18	111
Christian Democrats	10		7	42	4	30	3	10		106
Progressive Democrats		1	15			5				21
Conservatives		3							60	63
Liberals and Democrats	4	3	19	4		5	2	4		41
Independents & others	3	5			2	9		2	3*	24
Total	24	16	81	81	15	81	6	25	81	410

* 1 Scottish National Party, 1 Democratic Unionist, 1 Official Unionist

Turnout percentage	91.4	47.8	60.7	65.7	63.6	85.5	88.9	57.8	32.6	

Chapter 11
Political parties and general elections

Edmund Burke defined a political party as 'a body of men united for promoting by their joint endeavours the national interest, upon some particular principle in which they are all agreed'.

In Burke's time, the late-eighteenth century, parties existed only in Parliament. Our modern parties, with their mass membership, grew up about 100 years ago, when the vote was extended to most adult men. Women were kept waiting until 1918 and 1928. Political parties are now the link between us, the ordinary voters, and the Government—a link which becomes very clear during general elections.

What do the parties stand for?

Society changes and so do political parties, but their basic principles remain constant over many years. The way they apply these principles varies according to circumstances at a particular time.

There are several ways of finding out what political parties stand for. First, ask the parties themselves, nationally or locally. The London addresses of the main parties are given on page 127; a good reference library will supply the addresses of minor parties. Local and regional addresses are given in the telephone directory.

Try to get copies of the parties' last general election manifestos or more recent summaries of general policy. You could construct a

FOR ME, THE HEART OF POLITICS is not political theory, it is people and how they want to live their lives.

No one who has lived in this country during the last five years can fail to be aware of how the balance of our society has been increasingly tilted in favour of the State at the expense of individual freedom. . . .

It contains no magic formula or lavish promises. It is not a recipe for an easy or a perfect life. But it sets out a broad framework for the recovery of our country, based not on dogma, but on reason, on common sense, above all on the liberty of the people under the law.

The things we have in common as a nation far outnumber those that set us apart.

It is in that spirit that I commend to you this manifesto.

Margaret Thatcher

Our five tasks are:

1 To restore the health of our economic and social life, by controlling inflation and striking a fair balance between the rights and duties of the trade union movement.

2 To restore incentives so that hard work pays, success is rewarded and genuine new jobs are created in an expanding economy.

3 To uphold Parliament and the rule of law.

4 To support family life, by helping people to become home-owners, raising the standards of their children's education, and concentrating welfare services on the effective support of the old, the sick, the disabled and those who are in real need.

5 To strengthen Britain's defences and work with our allies to protect our interests in an increasingly threatening world.

This is the strategy of the next Conservative government.

chart, using the headings in Chapter 10, to compare their policies on current issues. This will show that they agree broadly about some problems and differ sharply about others. Even a party's most committed supporters are unlikely to agree with everything in its programme.

Secondly, find out what the two main parties have actually done when they were in power. This is much more difficult than reading manifestos. Most people form a general impression of Governments and rapidly forget the details.

Manifestos commit parties but any British Government is free to act differently—and sometimes has no choice. No Government has

Now, more than ever, we need Labour's traditional values of co-operation, social justice and fairness. This Manifesto re-states these Labour principles in an action programme with a strong sense of the future. They appeal to all our people—young and old . . . .
But although the 1980s will present a tough challenge, this country will have many things in our favour. North Sea oil offers a golden prospect as do our reserves of natural gas and coal. We must use these resources wisely to plan our future to create new wealth, new jobs, and to look after the family, the elderly and those in need . . . .

Here are five of our priorities.

One	We must keep a curb on inflation and prices . . . .
Two	We will carry forward the task of putting into practice the new framework to improve industrial relations that we have hammered out with the TUC . . . .
Three	We give high priority to working for a return to full employment . . . .
Four	We are deeply concerned to enlarge people's freedom . . . .
Five	We will use Britain's influence to strengthen world peace and defeat world poverty . . . .

The Labour Government will give a strong lead in the decade ahead. But no Government can do it all. Our purpose is to deepen the sense of unity and kinship and community feeling that has always marked out our fellow countrymen and women. No nation can succeed by accepting benefits without responsibilities. I ask everybody who shares our ideals and our faith in Britain to join with us in securing the return of a Government that dares to turn the dream of a caring society into practical action. And then work with us to complete the building of a Britain offering hope, social justice and fairness to all.

Jim Callaghan

1979 election manifestos of the major parties—introductions by the party leaders. What are the points of (a) similarity, (b) difference?

ever carried out all its party's manifesto promises, because they get knocked and buffeted by unforeseen happenings. The classical case was the repeal of the Corn Laws in 1846 by a Tory Prime Minister who had promised to keep them. A potato famine in Ireland knocked Peel off course—and his party split in two. Do you know any modern examples of startling 'U-turns'?

The following summary is a rough guide to the basic principles of the three main parties.

The Conservative Party.

'A living society can only change healthily when it changes naturally—that is, in accordance with its acquired and inherited character, and at a given rate ... Conservatives support the institution of private property and, in the main, the conduct of business through private enterprise.' (Quintin Hogg, *The Case for Conservatism.*)

Conservatives emphasize individual initiative and freedom from government interference. They believe in capitalism—the private ownership of industry, run at a profit for the shareholders. 'What we must continue to ensure is that any sacrifices are shared equitably and that hardship does not fall on those least able to bear it.' (*Conservative Manifesto*, February 1974.)

The Labour Party.

'To secure for the workers by hand or by brain the full fruits of their industry, and the most equitable distribution thereof that may be possible, upon the basis of the common ownership of the means of production, distribution, and exchange, and the best obtainable system of popular administration and control of each industry or service.' (Clause IV (4), *Party Constitution.*)

Socialists believe that increased public ownership and control of industry are essential to a fair distribution of wealth.

The Liberal Party.

'The great issue facing all nations in this century is how to combine the collective activity of the state, necessary for the welfare of the people, with democratic freedoms, and an opportunity for individual initiative in economic enterprise.' (*The Liberal Document*, September 1973.)

Liberals believe in a capitalist economic system and emphasize decentralization of political power and more participation by the people.

The Social Democratic Party

In 1981 this new party was founded by four ex-Labour Party ministers. They stated: 'We do not believe in the politics of an inert centre merely. representing the lowest common denominator between the two extremes. We want more, not less, radical change in our society, but with a greater stability of direction.' (*The Limehouse Declaration*, 25 January 1981).

The Social Democrats have entered into an alliance with the Liberals to fight by-elections and the next general election.

Party organization and finance

The object of the main parties is to win a majority of seats in Parliament and in local councils, in order to put their beliefs and principles into practice.

Party organization is based on constituencies; each constituency is represented by one Member of Parliament. The ordinary party member joins a smaller, local ward or polling district group; there are also special sections for women and young members. These groups and sections elect representatives to the constituency Executive Council (Conservatives) or General Management Committee (Labour). A constituency Labour party also has representatives from affiliated trade unions. Every party has representative district, regional or area committees.

The Annual Party Conferences in October are the highlights of the political year. Delegates, M.P.s and prospective candidates have a fine old time debating party policies. Not only in the Conference Hall, but also in cafes, bars and hotels, often late into the night. The rank-and-file constituency delegate breathes a heady, enthusiastic but sometimes controversial atmosphere.

The Labour and Liberal Conferences decide party policies. The Conservatives give their Leader power to decide policy; he listens carefully to what Conference has to say, as well as making at least one speech. The Labour Party manifesto is finally decided by a joint meeting of the National Executive Committee, elected by Conference, and the Parliamentary Committee, elected by Labour M.P.s.

Chapter 12 deals with party organization inside Parliament and the election of party leaders.

Every party needs money. At national level the Conservatives rely mainly on donations from business firms, the Labour Party on contributions from affiliated trade unions.

At local level all parties depend on members' subscriptions and donations, bingo, raffles, jumble sales, sweepstakes, bazaars, coffee mornings and evenings—and any other device they can think of for getting money out of supporters' pockets. They send some of it to their headquarters. Nearly all the Conservative constituency associations have a full-time paid agent and office staff. Less than half the Labour and Liberal constituency parties can afford them.

At Labour Party conferences delegates vote according to the number of members they represent. This card represents 1000 members

General elections

A general election must be held at least every five years, but a four years interval is more usual. The Prime Minister decides the date and tries to pick the most favourable time for his party. If his majority is very small (as in 1950 and 1964) or non-existent (as in February 1974) he finds it very difficult to carry on and 'goes to the country' within a year or two. A bye-election is held when an M.P. dies or resigns.

1979 General Election (Source: The Guardian, 3 May 1979)

General Elections 1945-79

	1945	1950	1951	1955	1959	1964	1966	1970	*(Feb)* 1974	*(Oct)* 1974	1979
Winning Party	Lab.	Lab.	Cons.	Cons.	Cons.	Lab.	Lab.	Cons.	–	Lab.	Cons.
Overall Majority	146	5	17	60	100	4	97	30	–	3	43
Seats Won											
Conservatives	213	298	321	345	365	303	253	330	296	276	339
Labour	393	315	295	277	258	317	363	287	301	319	268
Liberal	12	9	6	6	6	9	12	6	14	13	11
Others	22	3	3	2	1	1	2	7	24	27	17
Total	640	625	625	630	630	630	630	630	635	635	635
Percentage of votes											
Conservatives	39.9	43.5	48.0	49.7	49.3	43.4	41.9	46.4	38.1	35.7	43.9
Labour	48.0	46.1	48.8	46.4	43.8	44.1	47.9	42.9	37.2	39.3	36.9
Liberal	9.0	9.1	2.6	2.7	5.9	11.2	8.5	7.5	19.3	18.3	13.8
Others	3.1	1.3	0.7	1.2	1.0	1.3	1.7	3.2	5.4	6.7	5.4
Turnout percentage	76.1	84.0	82.5	76.8	78.8	77.0	75.8	71.4	78.7	72.8	76.0

General election time-table, May 1979

March 28	Labour Government defeated by one vote on Opposition vote of no confidence.
March 29	Prime Minister Callaghan advised Queen to dissolve Parliament.
March 30 —April 4	Parliament passed Interim Budget and law to hold General election and local elections on same day.
April 7	Dissolution of Parliament.
April 19	Last day for applications for postal and proxy votes.
April 23	Nominations for candidates closed at 3 p.m.
May 3	Polling Day, 7 a.m. to 10 p.m.
May 4	Final results announced. Mr Callaghan resigned. Mrs Thatcher became Prime Minister.
May 5	New Cabinet announced by Prime Minister.
May 9	New Parliament met to elect a Speaker and swear in Members.
May 12	State Opening of Parliament by the Queen.

The electoral system

'One adult, one vote.' The voter has a choice of at least two candidates. The candidate with the highest number of votes wins the seat; quite often he gets less than half the total votes.

The 635 constituencies vary in size, in spite of the efforts of impartial Boundary Commissions to make them roughly equal. In 1974 there were boundary changes in 435 constituencies. The average number of electors per seat was 58 000 in England, 50 000 in Wales, 48 000 in Scotland, 76 000 in Northern Ireland. Further changes will be made before the next general election (in 1983 or 1984?).

The electoral register is the same as for local elections and the rules about voting are very similar (see Chapter 4). The main differences are that

☐ peers *cannot* vote in general elections,

☐ people who have removed *can* apply for a postal vote.

Have another look at the official poll card and ballot paper on pages 25 and 27. In general elections the name of the constituency is printed at the top of the poll card.

Who can stand as a parliamentary candidate?

He or she must be a British subject, twenty-one years old or over. The candidate can live or work anywhere.

He or she must *not* be

☐ 'a holder of offices or places of profit under the Crown'; this rules out civil servants, judges, the police and armed forces, unless they first resign their jobs.

☐ a lunatic or peer

☐ a clergyman of the Church of England, Church of Scotland, or Roman Catholic Church.

As in local elections, bankrupts and people found guilty of 'corrupt or illegal practices' are disqualified.

Selection and nomination of parliamentary candidates

The majority of parliamentary candidates are selected by constituency associations/parties, often months or years before a general election. A sitting M.P. is usually chosen again, but his constituency party can, and sometimes does, refuse to re-adopt him. The Labour Party in 1980 decided that there must be a reselection before each general election.

Constituency parties please themselves whether to interview 'approved' candidates from the lists kept by party headquarters, or outsiders. In both cases names are sent in by the ward parties and sections. When a sitting M.P. retires from a safe seat dozens of names are put forward, because the selected candidate is almost sure to win the next election. A small constituency committee draws up a short-list of five or six names.

Then comes a special constituency selection meeting, which is great fun for the 50-60 party representatives who attend it, and probably slow torture for the would-be candidates. They make short speeches and answer questions in turn. (What questions would you ask?) The meeting decides which one to choose as prospective candidate. Normally he is then endorsed by party headquarters and begins to nurse the constituency.

The candidate is legally nominated about ten days before polling day, when he or his agent gives the Returning Officer at least one nomination paper signed by ten electors, and a deposit of £150. He will lose the deposit if he gets less than one-eighth of the total votes cast. This is supposed to deter 'frivolous' candidates and the amount of the deposit is likely to be substantially increased before the first general election in the 1980s.

The election campaign at national level

The campaign is short, sharp and hectic—only three or four weeks. Each national party publishes its manifesto a day or two after the election date is announced. It is a summary of what the party hopes to do if it wins the election. Then comes a spate of posters and leaflets, summarizing the manifesto or dealing with particular issues, such as prices. There is no legal limit on a party's national expenses, although each candidate is strictly limited in the amount he or she can spend on the campaign.

Television and radio programmes probably have a bigger impact on voters than election 'literature'. Only a determined 'knob-twiddler' can avoid political news, discussions, interviews and party broadcasts during an election campaign. The BBC and television companies are legally obliged to treat the parties and candidates impartially, but minor parties always claim that they don't get enough time. There is research evidence that the programmes change very few voting intentions, although they do make people better informed about election issues and the personalities of party leaders.

82

The newspapers are not impartial, as you can easily discover by comparing their headlines and comments on the same speech. Since 1959 the main parties have held morning press conferences in London. The national newspapers send reporters to tail the leaders as they make speeches at big public meetings all over the country and go on 'walk-abouts' to meet the people—if they can get near them through the posse of policemen and reporters. Indoor meetings are likely to be attended only by party supporters and determined 'hecklers'.

Campaign polls: general election 1979—final predictions

Fieldwork	Publication		Poll	Cons. %	Lab. %	Lib. %	Other %	Cons. % Lead	Sample size
	Date	Place							
29 Apr.-1 May	3 May	*Express*	MORI	44.4	38.8	13.5	3.3	5.6	947
1 May	3 May	*Sun*	MARPLAN	45	38.5	13.5	3	6.5	1 973
1-2 May	3 May	*Mail*	NOP	46	39	12.5	2.5	7	1 069
1-2 May	3 May	*Telegraph*	GALLUP	43	41	13.5	2.5	2	2 348
2 May	3 May	*Evening Standard*	MORI	45	37	15	3	8	1 089
			Actual result	44.9	37.7	14.1	3.3	7.2	

(Source: D. Butler and D. Kavanagh: The British General Election of 1979, Macmillan, 1980)

In one or two earlier general elections polls made faulty predictions. But in 1979 they were remarkably accurate. The nearer the interviews are to polling day the more accurate they are likely to be. It is easier to forecast the total vote for a party than the number of seats they are likely to win. How do you explain this? Do you think that opinion polls have any effect on the voters during an election campaign? Should they be banned by law as in some other countries?

The election campaign at constituency level

The campaign is run on a bigger scale than at local elections. More public meetings, more leaflets to be stuffed in letter boxes, more canvassing—and fortunately more party workers offering their unpaid services.

The candidate's first job is to write the election address, including points from the party manifesto. Each candidate is allowed one free postal delivery, which is generally used to get the election address into every home.

In the mornings he sees local press reporters, deals with urgent correspondence and questionnaires from pressure groups, and discusses plans with his agent. Then off he goes to meet as many voters as possible; canvassing with party workers, factory gate and shopping centre meetings, indoor meetings, visiting clubs and old people's homes. By polling day his voice has become a hoarse croak.

CORRUPT PRACTICES

Bribery, i.e., giving or promising to any person any money or anything valuable with the object of securing his or somebody else's vote.

Any person who receives a bribe, or bargains for employment or reward, in consideration of his vote, is guilty of bribery.

Treating, i.e., giving food, drink or entertainment to a person with the object of securing his or somebody else's vote. (Remember that the standing of a single drink may be "treating" if it is done with this object in view).

The receiver of any meal, drink, etc., is equally guilty, and liable to the same consequences.

Undue influence, i.e., threatening any sort of harm to a person to induce him to vote or not to vote for a particular candidate.

The withdrawal of custom, or a threat to do so, comes under this prohibition. A threat to evict a tenant will also be undue influence.

Incurring unauthorised expenses, i.e., incurring, without having been PREVIOUSLY authorised by me IN WRITING to do so, any expense in holding a public meeting, organising a public display, issuing any advertisement, circular or publication (except in a newspaper) or otherwise presenting to the electors the candidate or his views to the extent or nature of his backing or disparaging any other candidate.

Personation, i.e., applying to vote in the name of some other person or attempting to persuade another person to do so.

The punishment for a corrupt practice, other than personation, is a year's imprisonment or a fine of £200 and, for personation, two years' imprisonment; in both cases the offender is disqualified for five years for voting at any parliamentary or local government election in Great Britain, for being a member of the House of Commons or of a local authority and for holding any judicial office.

ILLEGAL PRACTICES

Paying any money provided for election expenses to any person except the candidate or myself.

Paying any election expenses except through me.

Agreeing to pay a voter for the exhibition of election notices unless the voter ordinarily carried on business as an advertising agent.

Making a false statement about the PERSONAL character or conduct of another candidate.

Interrupting another candidate's meeting by disorderly conduct or inciting another person to do so.

Inducing a voter to vote when he is under a legal incapacity to do so, e.g., because he is under eighteen; or to vote in person when he is entitled to vote by post or by proxy.

Paying for the conveyance of a voter to or from the poll; or conveying him to or from the poll in ANY vehicle which is ordinarily kept for hire.

The punishment of an illegal practice is a fine of £100 and the offender is disqualified for five years for voting at any parliamentary or local government election in the constituency or in any part of it.

No PAID assistant may canvass.

REQUIREMENT OF SECRECY

Any person acting in contravention of R.P. Act, 1949, Section 53, in respect of secrecy requirements at the Poll, Count or at the issue and receipt of Postal Vote Ballot Papers.

To the offenders, up to six months imprisonment.

Summary of election laws warning the agent against bribery and corruption

Polling day

A parliamentary candidate with his agent

The election agent organizes the motley band of volunteer workers and looks after legal forms and accounts. He reckons that if the canvassers find 20 000-22 000 'promises' of support, the candidate will get 16 000-17 000 actual votes. Some'voters do not tell the truth and some canvassers are too optimistic.

We have had very strict laws against bribery and corruption of voters since 1883. The agent is responsible and can be sent to prison if these laws are broken. He must also try to stop young members tearing down opponents' posters and fly-posting their own.

On polling day the polling stations are open from 7 a.m. to 10 p.m., a heavy strain on officials and party workers. But voters have more time and need less persuasion to turn out than in local elections, so 'knocking-up' is easier, even if it snows.

In towns the count normally takes place the same night. Rural constituencies have to leave it till the next morning.

Why do people vote the way they do?

Here are some explanations given by political researchers, who have tried to solve the question by sample surveys.

We are all politically influenced, often unconsciously, by the family we grow up in, by our income and the kind of work we do, by colleagues at work, and by the neighbourhood we live in.

In every general election between 1945 and October 1974 a majority of men voted Labour. For the first time in 1979 more voted Conservative. Apart from 1945 and 1966 a majority of women voted for the Conservatives. (Does this tell us anything important about voting behaviour?)

Young people tend to be less conservative than the elderly, but they also tend to vote the same way as their parents.

Some people adopt a political philosophy or attitude when they are young and stick to it all their lives. Others change their minds from one election to another. It is very difficult to calculate how

85

many, because a lot of the changes cancel one another out, leaving a small net swing between the main parties.

It used to be said that nearly all changes of opinion happened between general elections. It now seems clear that swings occurred towards the end of the 1970 and both 1974 campaigns. Or perhaps an unusually high number of puzzled and undecided people made up their minds in the last day or two. Whatever the reasons, the results of all three elections were a surprise.

It is clear that the personality of a candidate is less important to the majority of voters than the party he represents. There is some evidence, however, that this *can* make a crucial difference, especially in 'marginal' constituencies. However good the organization is it cannot make more than a dent in a constituency where one party has an enormous majority, but in a closely fought race it could be the decisive factor. Experienced agents swear that a well-respected, sitting M.P. attracts more votes than a new candidate, and that a well-organized campaign increases the turn-out and makes a vital difference in marginal seats.

You could learn something by asking people how and why they voted at the last general election. Or why they didn't vote. They will give you the reason which is uppermost in their minds, or tell you that voting is secret! You will find very few who solemnly read all the party manifestos and then decided how to vote.

How do young people vote?

Here are the results of an opinion poll taken by Marplan for the *News of the World* on 18–22-year-olds at the beginning of the general election campaign in 1979. Twenty per cent of them were still undecided; the rest said they would vote as below.

47%   5%   45%

	All young voters (%)	Men only (%)	Women only (%)
Conservative	47	44	51
Labour	45	48	41
Liberal	5	5	6
Others	3	4	3

An unfair voting system?

The British voting system does not reflect accurately the number of votes cast for each party. Since 1945 the Liberals and minor parties have always got a lower percentage of seats than of votes. Nor does the party which gets the most votes always get the most seats in Parliament (1951 and February, 1974).

So ought we to change to a system of 'proportional representa-

Getting ready to count the votes.
Lambeth Town Hall, May 1979

tion' which would give all parties a share of the seats nearly in proportion to their popular support? There are several variations of P.R., widely used in Western Europe. The Electoral Reform Society and the Liberal Party favour the *single transferable vote*. This

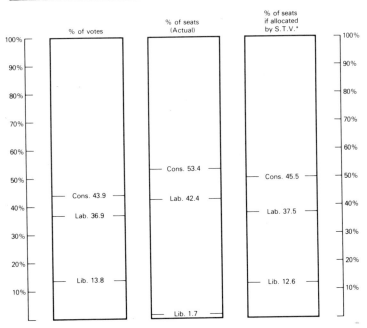

An unfair voting system? General election, 1979

Source: D. Butler and D. Kavanagh: The British General Election of 1979, Macmillan, 1980

system has been used in Northern Ireland and the Kilbrandon Commission recommended it for Scottish and Welsh Assemblies.

How does it work? Instead of single-member constituencies there are large constituencies, each returning five or six M.P.s. Instead of placing an X on the ballot paper, the voter numbers the candidates in order of preference, 1, 2, 3, and so on. Each successful candidate must obtain a 'quota' of votes:

$$\left(\frac{\text{total votes cast}}{\text{number of seats} + 1} \right) + 1$$

When a candidate gets more than the quota, the second preferences on his ballot papers are transferred to the other candidates. The candidates with least votes have them transferred to the others. This goes on until five (or six) candidates have reached the quota.

The *regional list* system of P.R. divides a country into large regional constituencies. In each region the parties choose their own lists of candidates, matching the number of seats. The voter gets a large ballot paper, with each party's list running horizontally across the paper. He votes for only one candidate in one party. Suppose there are four seats in one region. If Party A gets half the total votes, it gets two seats for its two most popular candidates. In practice it is never as simple as that; there are several methods of sharing the seats in proportion to the votes, as nearly as possible. Other varieties of proportional representation include the *alternative vote, second ballot, national party list* and additional member systems.

Our present system is certainly unfair to small parties and the voters who support them. On the other hand, people are primarily voting for the next Government. No political party has got more than half the votes since 1935. If the elections had been fought under a proportional representation system it is unlikely that any party would have won a clear majority of seats. That is why the Conservative and Labour Parties prefer our present system, which usually produces clear majorities for one of them. They do not want their hands to be tied in Government by coalitions or agreements with smaller parties which do not share their views and policies.

What do you think?

Chapter 12
Parliament

A recent exhausting general election is over. After a few days' rest the newly elected Members go to the House of Commons for the preliminary ceremonies.

Election of the Speaker

First, the M.P.s elect their chairman, Mr Speaker. They choose an experienced M.P. whom they trust to supervise debates impartially. Traditionally he is dragged reluctantly to the Chair by the proposer and seconder. This is a reminder that in the old days he had the often dangerous job of acting as the Commons' spokesman in struggles with powerful kings and queens. The Speaker 'swears in' the other Members.

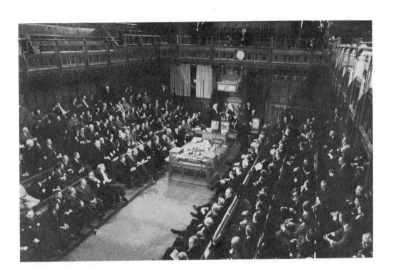

Inside the House of Commons, Mr Speaker in the Chair

The Speaker must know the Standing Orders (rules of procedure) as thoroughly as a World Cup referee knows the rules of football. In the Chamber he keeps debates orderly, selects speakers, and calls them to order if they stray from the subject.

When a new Parliament meets there is another reminder of old battles with the Crown. The Speaker formally claims the hard-won rights of M.P.s: freedom of speech, freedom from arrest (except on criminal charges), the right to make their own rules and decide their own parliamentary business, and the power to punish outsiders for 'breach of privilege', such as threatening M.P.s or disobeying Orders of the House.

The House of Commons sits continuously from 2.30 p.m. to 10.30 p.m., except on Fridays, (9.30 a.m. to 2.30 p.m.) so the Speaker needs a Deputy to relieve him. He also leaves the Chair when they meet more informally as a Committee of the Whole House.

Outside the debating Chamber the Speaker has several duties. He issues writs for bye-elections, receives messages from M.P.s who would like to speak in debates, decides which amendments to motions (proposals) shall be debated, represents the Commons at various functions, and presides over the Speaker's Conference on electoral reform. Do you know the name of the present Speaker?

The State Opening of Parliament

This ancient ceremony comes a few days after the election of the Speaker, and also every November at the beginning of a new session. All three historic parts of Parliament are involved—the Monarch, the House of Lords, the House of Commons. And the Yeomen of the Guard still search the cellars of Parliament in case another Guy Fawkes is lurking there with modern gelignite.

The Queen usually drives from Buckingham Palace in an open coach, wearing a crown, and sits on her throne in the House of Lords. In front of her sit the peers and peeresses, judges and ambassadors, in splendid robes. Crowded at the entrance are the people who matter politically—the Prime Minister, the Leader of the Opposition, and as many M.P.s as can get their noses in.

The Queen then reads the 'Queen's speech', which is actually written by the Prime Minister and approved by the Cabinet. It is a

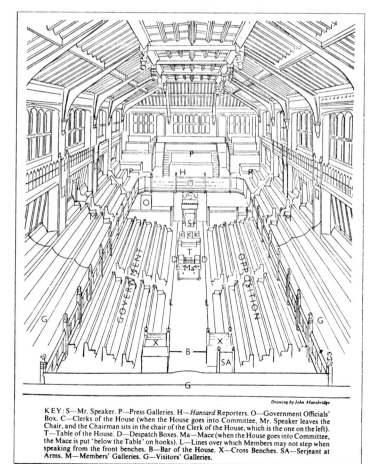

Drawing by John Mansbridge

Plan of the Chamber of the House of Commons

KEY: S—Mr. Speaker. P—Press Galleries. H—*Hansard* Reporters. O—Government Officials' Box. C—Clerks of the House (when the House goes into Committee, Mr. Speaker leaves the Chair, and the Chairman sits in the chair of the Clerk of the House, which is the one on the left). T—Table of the House. D—Despatch Boxes. Ma—Mace (when the House goes into Committee, the Mace is put 'below the Table' on hooks). L—Lines over which Members may not step when speaking from the front benches. B—Bar of the House. X—Cross Benches. SA—Serjeant at Arms. M—Members' Galleries. G—Visitors' Galleries.

summary of what the Government intends to do during the coming session. The debate on this speech is the first round in each new session of Parliament.

The work of a Member of Parliament

What is it like to be an M.P.? I put the following questions to a Member who was first elected in 1955 and represents a constituency near Manchester.

Are you a full-time M.P.?   Yes. I don't believe it's possible to do the job properly if you have a part-time job as well.

What do you do on a typical day in the House of Commons?   No two days are alike, but I go to the House about 8.45 a.m. and leave

State Opening of Parliament, the House of Lords

91

ORAL ANSWERS TO QUESTIONS

EDUCATION AND SCIENCE
School Transport

1. Dr. Edmund Marshall asked the Secretary of State for Education and Science what is his policy in respect of the recommendations of the working party on school transport.

24. Mr. Milne asked the Secretary of State for Education and Science what action he proposes to take on the report on school transport and bus travel arrangements.

The Secretary of State for Education and Science (Mr. Reg Prentice): I hope soon to have the views of the local authority associations on the report of the working party on school transport. When I have received and considered their views I shall make a statement.

Dr. Marshall: May I impress upon my right hon. Friend the urgency with which some of my constituents regard the matter? When he is formulating proposals, will he ensure that no parent is required to pay more towards the cost of his child's transport to school than is incurred already?

Mr. Prentice: I am aware of the urgency of the matter and of the particular concern arising from the tragic deaths as a result of the accident which my hon. Friend drew to my predecessor's attention. I do not want to anticipate decisions on the report, which is complicated, and I shall need to have the views of local authorities before making a statement.

Mr. Redmond: While making no party point on this subject, and realising that the right hon. Gentleman has had only four weeks in his Department, may I ask whether he does not think that this matter has been hanging about long enough and that it is time we had an urgent decision? Would it not be better to get on with this matter than decide about comprehensive schools?

Mr. Prentice: It is very important to get on with the question of comprehensive schools. However, I believe that this

Extract from Hansard, 2 April 1974
Note: Mr. Prentice provides an example of the exception to the general rule. He left the Labour Party, became a Conservative M.P. and was appointed as a minister by Mrs. Thatcher.

at 10.45 p.m. In the mornings I answer some of my letters (30 or 40 a day), read the newspapers, and dip into Hansard, which is the official word-for-word report of the previous day's speeches. On Tuesday or Thursday mornings I attend a Standing Committee from 10.30 to one o'clock. Some Members are on Select Committees as well. Sometimes I prepare a speech and do research in the Library.

I have lunch in the cafeteria or a snack in the tea-room; the Members' Dining Room is very grand but rather expensive. The House meets at 2.30 and I stay in the Chamber till about five o'clock, for Question Time and the opening speeches by Ministers and Opposition spokesmen in the main debate.

For the next four hours it varies—writing more letters, attending party meetings or lectures by outside experts, exchanging views informally with colleagues. I meet deputations and get visitors from all over the country and indeed the world. Sometimes there are constituents who've asked me to get them tickets for the Visitors' Gallery.

At nine o'clock I go back into the Chamber, listen to the closing Front Bench speeches and vote in the division at ten o'clock. I usually stay for the half-hour adjournment debate, when back-bench M.P.s raise constituency or individual problems and a Junior Minister answers them. After that I walk back to my digs with friends, still arguing, and get to bed at midnight.

What happens at Question Time? It's a magnificent opportunity to question a Minister on any matter for which he is responsible, and demand an answer. We give a few days' notice and the questions are printed on the Order Paper, our daily agenda. The Minister reads his prepared answer, but we can put another supplementary question orally. He doesn't know what that will be, though his civil service advisers try to guess and brief him with suitable answers. It's like a game of chess, but deadly serious and done at great speed—up to fifty questions and fifty supplementaries in less than an hour. On Tuesdays and Thursdays the Prime Minister answers questions for fifteen minutes. Do I ask questions only when my party is in Opposition? Oh no, I question any Minister who sends me an unsatisfactory reply to my letters about constituency grievances, or about policy.

How often do you speak in debates? Two or three times a year. When I was a new M.P. I prepared a lot of speeches and sat solidly through long debates, bobbing up every time a speech finished and trying to catch the Speaker's eye. But he hardly ever called me and it was very wearing and frustrating. Now I specialize, mainly on housing and foreign policy, and when I do get up the Speaker gives me a fair deal.

Why are there only a few M.P.s in the Chamber in the evening? Three reasons. Firstly, we'd go round the bend if we listened to speeches for hours at a time. Secondly, we've got a lot of other work to do. Thirdly, some of the speeches and subjects are very boring. There is a quorum of forty, but the Speaker doesn't enforce this rule unless a Member draws his attention to it. (*Note*: Changes have since been made and the quorum applies only to certain items of business.)

There are closed circuit television sets in all the main rooms, which announce the name of the speaker who has the floor, so we have an idea what's going on. If the Prime Minister or Leader of the Opposition comes up you'll soon see us striding back to the Chamber. Some of us go up to the Members' Galleries, because there are only 346 seats for 635 M.P.s.

Why does the House sometimes have all-night sittings? Because there's so much business to get through. It's not as bad as it used to be. At one time we debated the lengthy Finance Bill in the Chamber, as a Committee of the Whole House, in great detail. Now parts of it go upstairs to a Standing Committee, which saves time.

What is a 'division'? How do M.P.s vote? The division bells ring throughout the building when a vote is going to be taken. We rush into the Chamber and vote by walking through the Aye Lobby or No Lobby—corridors which run each side of the Speaker's Chair. Our names are ticked off by Tellers, who give the result to the Speaker. Each vote takes about ten minutes.

Is it true that M.P.s always vote according to party instructions?
Not always. There are 'free' votes on matters of personal conscience, such as divorce laws. Otherwise a lot depends on the Government's position. If their majority is tiny, or even no majority at all, their M.P.s nearly always support them. Defeat on a vote of confidence means the Government's resignation and almost certainly a general election. When the majority is big, party discipline is less strict. Then a small group of M.P.s who disagree sometimes vote against their own party on important issues, or more likely abstain.

How are parties organized in Parliament? The Parliamentary Labour Party includes all Labour M.P.s and peers. There's a private meeting once a week to thrash out differences of opinion, and several subject groups to study things like foreign policy and defence in detail. The PLP elects a Parliamentary Committee which is the Shadow Cabinet of leading spokesmen when Labour is in opposition. The Conservative 1922 Committee is a private meeting of backbenchers only, though they sometimes invite Ministers to attend. Labour and Conservative M.P.s elect their Party Leaders. But Labour may change to election by the whole Party membership, as the Liberals did in 1976. (A new system for electing the Leader and Deputy-Leader of the Labour Party is to operate from 1981. These are to be chosen by an electoral college in which the Parliamentary Party, the constituency parties and the trade unions each have one-third of the votes.)

All parties appoint *Whips*, who try to ensure a maximum party vote in the House, especially on vital issues. On Fridays we get a list of the next week's business from our own Chief Whip. He underlines each expected division with one, two or three lines. A three-line whip means we must be there to vote. Two lines means that we can 'pair' with an M.P. of the opposite party, if both of us have to be absent. One line means that it isn't important.

The Whips keep in close touch with back-benchers and know what we're grumbling and worrying about. Some people call us 'lobby-fodder', but Governments have been known to change their plans because their own back-benchers wouldn't wear them.

What do you do at weekends?   I go home to Manchester on Friday or Thursday evening. More letters are waiting for me and a list of engagements—constituency and ward party meetings, functions and conferences of all kinds. Twice a month I hold 'surgeries' on Sunday mornings. I spend a lot of time listening to people's views and worries. I try to keep Saturdays free for my family, but that rule gets broken when I'm invited to speak in other parts of the country.

How can you help constituents with personal problems?   They write to me or come to the Sunday surgeries. My constituency has a lot of bad housing and endless poverty problems. 'We've been on the council's housing list ten years.' 'The roof's leaking and the landlord won't mend it.' 'I can't keep up with my mortgage payments.' Sometimes I can help by writing to the District Council's Housing Manager or public health inspectors. But housing problems like these need a much bigger house-building programme and better Housing and Rent Acts. I campaign for them inside and outside Parliament.

I see deserted wives who are getting no maintenance from their husbands, elderly pensioners trying to manage without supplementary benefit, prisoners' wives and mothers near the end of their tether. I explain what government departments can do for them. If civil servants seem to be at fault I write to their Minister, knowing that he will order an investigation. Truly, one half of the world doesn't know how the other half lives.

How do you learn about constituency grievances?   People stop me

The Disablement Incomes Group present petitions to their M.P.s outside Parliament

Central Lobby of the Houses of Parliament

in the street, tell me at meetings, or write long letters. Deputations come up to London and 'lobby' me in the House. One day there's a group of shop stewards, alarmed by threats of redundancy or closure of their factory. Next day a deputation of local councillors seeking my support for higher grants before they descend in wrath on a Minister. I must use my own judgement, but I certainly back constituency groups with all my weight when I believe they're right.

Like all M.P.s I get letters and circulars every day from national pressure groups. In the same post we may be asked to support both teetotallers and brewers.

Is it true that M.P.s.' working conditions are bad?　No, I don't think so. Bad conditions have been exaggerated and conditions have been improved lately. I've got a desk and my own portable typewriter in a room which I share with seven other Members. It's usually only Ministers and Opposition leading spokesmen who get a room of their own. Most of us do our own research, with some help from party Head Offices. (M.P.s now receive an allowance for secretarial *and* research help. See below.)

How much do M.P.s earn?　£6270 in 1977/8, plus an allowance to cover the extra expense of living in London midweek (for provincial M.P.s) and for secretarial help. There are deductions for income tax, national insurance, and pension contributions. (M.P.s salaries were increased to £13,950 p.a. in June 1981.)

What does 'disclosing financial interests' mean?　'Financial interests' are all non-Parliamentary sources of income. A Member must tell the House about any relevant financial interest before he speaks in debates and committees or asks questions. In May 1974, the House decided that there should be a compulsory register of interests, which any member of the public can examine.

What do you think is the main job of an M.P.?　To press the

95

Government for the best possible policies. By the best policies I mean those a Member believes to be in the interests of the majority of the people and of his constituents. Usually they are what have been outlined in his election address or his Party's manifesto. Sometimes there are difficult conflicting loyalties.

Functions of Parliament

Parliament has three main functions—to pass laws, to watch and criticize the Government, and to control the raising and spending of money.

How a Bill becomes an Act

New laws are called Bills until they are finally passed and become Acts. There are three main kinds of Bills.

ELIZABETH II

Education (School-leaving Dates) Act 1976

1976 CHAPTER 5

An Act to make further provision with respect to school-leaving dates; and for connected purposes.
[25th March 1976]

BE IT ENACTED by the Queen's most Excellent Majesty, by and with the advice and consent of the Lords Spiritual and Temporal, and Commons, in this present Parliament assembled, and by the authority of the same, as follows:—

1.—(1) For subsections (3) and (4) of section 9 of the Education Act 1962 (under which a person who attains the age of 16 between the end of January and the beginning of September is deemed to attain the upper limit of compulsory school age at the end of the summer term) there shall be substituted— *Alteration of summer school-leaving date. 1962 c. 12.*

"(3) If he attains that age after the end of January but before the next May school-leaving date, he shall be deemed not to have attained that age until that date.

(4) If he attains that age after the May school-leaving date and before the beginning of September next following that date, he shall be deemed to have attained that age on that date."

(2) After subsection (7) of that section there shall be added—
"(8) In this section "the May school-leaving date" means the Friday before the last Monday in May."

2.—(1) The power to make regulations under section 13 of the Family Allowances Act 1965 shall include power to provide that a person who has attained the upper limit of compulsory school age for the purposes of that Act shall be treated for those purposes as being under that limit until such date as may be specified in the regulations; and regulations made by virtue of this subsection may make different provision for different cases. *Family allowances and social security. 1965 c. 53.*

LOCAL GOVERNMENT IN ENGLAND

GOVERNMENT PROPOSALS FOR REORGANISATION

I. INTRODUCTION AND BACKGROUND

Essential Purpose of the Present White Paper

1. The structure of local government in England is that which was bequeathed to us by the legislation of 1888 and 1894. At that time there were no motor cars on our roads; there was no electricity in our homes; and the population of England was less than 28 millions. It is therefore understandable that for more than a quarter of a century proposals for the reorganisation of local government have been under discussion. The magnitude of the problems of the remainder of the 20th century is such that reorganisation is now urgent.

2. In 1963/65 a major reform of London Government was undertaken and completed. In 1966 a Royal Commission was set up under the chairmanship of Lord Redcliffe-Maud to examine the problems of local government in the rest of England, local authority associations and a wide range of observers all agreeing on the need for reform. The report of the Royal Commission* was published in 1969 and their proposals together with the related research studies have provoked considerable debate and discussion.

3. At the last General Election all three major parties were committed to pursue policies of major local government reform and the Conservative Party pledged themselves to introduce a system of two-tier government rationalising the operation of the various functions. Local government provides vital services on which the quality of social and economic life in this country depends. It is an essential part of the whole democratic framework of Government. The interests of local government as a whole will best be served by ending the period of uncertainty which has hung over local authorities, their members and officers for so long. The time has come for decision and action.

4. The purpose of this White Paper is, therefore, two-fold. First, to outline the structural changes which the Government believe to be necessary to fulfil their election pledges, these pledges having been made after carefully considering the findings of the Royal Commission, Mr. Senior's dissenting memorandum, the multitude of other proposals propounded both before and after the Commission had reported, and the reactions and views of the local authorities and their associations. And secondly, to indicate the proposed timing of legislation and of final implementation.

Objectives of Reform

5. Without doubt the opportunities for local authorities to take the vital decisions that affect their areas are more exciting now than at any other time. The pace of change and the scale of technological control over that change is such that men and women in local government can influence the environment in which they and their children will live in a way that has never been

* The Report of the Royal Commission on Local Government in England (Cmnd 4040)

Above left: First page of the Education (School-leaving Dates) Act 1976

Above right: Extract from Government White Paper, February 1971

1   *Public Bills* are put forward by the Government and steered through Parliament by the Ministers in charge of them. (There is more about the Minister's part in Chapter 14.)

Sometimes the proposals are first set out in a White Paper,

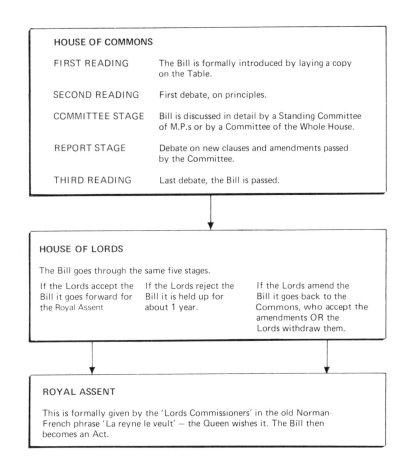

How a Bill becomes an Act

HOUSE OF COMMONS

FIRST READING	The Bill is formally introduced by laying a copy on the Table.
SECOND READING	First debate, on principles.
COMMITTEE STAGE	Bill is discussed in detail by a Standing Committee of M.P.s or by a Committee of the Whole House.
REPORT STAGE	Debate on new clauses and amendments passed by the Committee.
THIRD READING	Last debate, the Bill is passed.

HOUSE OF LORDS

The Bill goes through the same five stages.

If the Lords accept the Bill it goes forward for the Royal Assent	If the Lords reject the Bill it is held up for about 1 year.	If the Lords amend the Bill it goes back to the Commons, who accept the amendments OR the Lords withdraw them.

ROYAL ASSENT

This is formally given by the 'Lords Commissioners' in the old Norman-French phrase 'La reyne le veult' — the Queen wishes it. The Bill then becomes an Act.

which has been approved by the Cabinet and later debated in Parliament. Then the detailed Bill is drafted by specialized civil servants called Parliamentary Counsel to the Treasury, who try to make the wording exact and legally watertight. The Cabinet decides the Bill's place in the Parliamentary queue.

The chart above shows the main stages through which the Bill has to pass. The debates about it in the House of Commons are sometimes cut short by *closure*. The Government Chief Whip moves 'that the question be now put' and a vote is taken if 100 M.P.s support him and the Speaker approves. If a Bill is very long and controversial the Government often uses the *guillotine* in the Standing Committee. Each part of the Bill is allotted so much time and the knife falls even if some clauses have not been discussed at all.

2 *Private Members' Bills* are introduced on Fridays by back-benchers who have won a high place in the ballot for precious time. The Abolition of Capital Punishment Act and the Abortion Act were introduced by private Members; in both cases there was a free vote. M.P.s also ballot for permission to introduce a Ten Minute Rule Bill during the week. They have ten minutes to propose it, a useful way of publicizing their views, even if it gets no further.

3   *Private Bills* are promoted by local councils, public corporations and other bodies which want extra powers. They do not apply to the whole country. These Bills go through a special procedure and get quick final approval by the House of Commons, as you can see in the 'typical day' time-table.

A typical day in the House of Commons Chamber

2.30	Prayers.
2.35	Preliminary business, for example, new writs for bye-elections, unopposed Private Bills, public petitions.
2.45	Questions to Ministers from M.P.s of all parties.
3.30	'Private notice' questions (urgent). Brief statements and discussion on exceptional matters, for example, Prime Minister's statement about an international crisis. Ten Minute Rule Bills introduced by back-bench M.P.s.
3.45	Public business begins—debates on Bills or on general policy matters.
7.00	Possible interruption of public business to deal with other matters.
10.00	Main debate ends with a division, unless the debate is to be continued on a second day. This is often followed by a 'debate on the adjournment', when back-bench M.P.s raise grievances and get a reply from a junior Minister.
10.30	The House adjourns. If business is very heavy the House sometimes continues until the next morning.

Delegated legislation   Many Acts of Parliament are fairly short, but they give a Minister power to make detailed rules and orders (known as Statutory Instruments) or to approve local bye-laws. The House of Commons gets an opportunity to criticize and reject important Statutory Instruments, but there is hardly ever time to examine them thoroughly.

The House of Commons as watchdog and critic

Parliament originally won its power to criticize the King and his Ministers by refusing to vote them new taxes until they put an end to grievances. (More about this financial weapon in Chapter 15.)

Today the opposition M.P.s act as the Government's main critics. The Leader of the Opposition is paid a salary in recognition of the importance of this role. But M.P.s of all parties are critical. The Government is often reproached by its own supporters for not going far enough, or for going too far.

How do M.P.s act as watchdogs? As we have seen, they speak in debates on White Papers and Bills. In addition, on 'Supply Days' the Opposition can decide the subject for debate. Back-benchers bring all kinds of grievances to light in the short adjournment debates after 10 p.m., as well as harrying Ministers at Question Time and proposing their own Bills and critical motions.

1977 No. 764

PROTECTION OF WRECKS

The Protection of Wrecks (Designation No. 1) Order 1977

Made - - - -	*29th April* 1977
Laid before Parliament	*6th May* 1977
Coming into Operation	*27th May* 1977

The Secretary of State, being satisfied that the site identified in article 2 of this Order is the site of a vessel lying wrecked on the sea bed and that on account of the historical and archaeological importance of the vessel the site ought to be protected from unauthorised interference, after consulting with the persons referred to in section 1(4) of the Protection of Wrecks Act 1973(a), in exercise of the powers conferred on him by section 1(1), (2) and (4) of that Act and all other powers enabling him in that behalf, hereby orders as follows:—

1.—(1) This Order may be cited as the Protection of Wrecks (Designation No. 1) Order 1977 and shall come into operation on 27th May 1977.

(2) The Interpretation Act 1889(b) shall apply for the interpretation of this Order as it applies for the interpretation of an Act of Parliament.

2. The site in respect of which this Order is made is hereby identified as the site where a vessel lies wrecked on the sea bed at Latitude 51° 31′ 44″ North, Longitude 01° 14′ 53″ East.

3. The area within a distance of 100 metres of Latitude 51° 31′ 44″ North, Longitude 01° 14′ 53″ East shall be a restricted area for the purposes of the Protection of Wrecks Act 1973.

29th April 1977.

Stanley Clinton Davis,
Parliamentary Under-Secretary of State,
Department of Trade.

EXPLANATORY NOTE

(*This Note is not part of the Order.*)

This Order designates as a restricted area for the purpose of the Protection of Wrecks Act 1973 an area in the South Edinburgh Channel, Thames Estuary, round the site of the wreck of a vessel which is of historical importance.

(a) 1973 c. 33.   (b) 1889 c. 63.

Select Committees

Liaison Committee

Selection Committee

Departmental Committees
    Agriculture
    Defence
    Education, Science and
    Arts
    Energy
    Environment
    Foreign Affairs
    Home Affairs
    Industry and Trade
    Scottish Affairs
    Social Services
    Transport
    Treasury and Civil Service
    Welsh Affairs

Public Accounts Committee

Statutory Instruments
Committee

Committee on European
Legislation

Parliamentary Commissioner for
Administration Committee

The House of Commons has an elaborate system of committees which meet in rooms upstairs. Most of them are another means of probing Government intentions and deeds.

Standing Committees of between thirty and fifty Members from all parties examine most public Bills in detail.

Select Committees A new system of committees, designed to achieve a more searching and effective check on Government policy and administration, was established in 1979. These are small committees, with between nine and thirteen members, which are entitled to demand information and to interview Ministers and civil servants. There are now fourteen 'departmental' committees plus four retained from the earlier structure. Additionally there is a Liaison Committee which maintains a general oversight of the committees and a Selection Committee which arranges the membership. The committees produce reports which are debated in the House of Commons and important findings are likely to be publicized in the newspapers and on television.

Critics of our system say that a lot of this is eye-wash. 'If the Government has a clear majority it can get almost anything through Parliament and all this criticism doesn't make much difference.' Even if this were true, there is always a general election looming a-head. Opposition M.P.s are often talking indirectly to the people and putting their case to form the next Government. It has often been argued that the proceedings of the House of Commons should be televised but following votes, M.P.s turned the idea down in 1966, 1972 and 1975. But radio broadcasts started, as an experiment, on 9 June 1975. Broadcasts of Prime Minister's Question Time and some important debates started in 1978. Extracts are used in news programmes on radio and television (sound only).

The House of Lords

The Upper House is an undemocratic survival of the past and occupies half the Parliament building. Since 1911 there have been changes in its membership and powers.

1911 Parliament Act took away its power to reject Money Bills. The Lords could delay other Public Bills two years but not reject them indefinitely.

1949 Parliament Act reduced the Lords' delaying power to one year.

1958 Peerage Act made it possible to create life peers, including women, whose titles died with them.

1963 Peerage Act allowed hereditary peers to renounce their titles and seek election to the House of Commons. Lord Stansgate, who fought for the Act, became Anthony Wedgwood Benn again.

Since 1964 no new hereditary peerages have been created. By 1980 the House of Lords had nearly 1200 members: about 800 hereditary peers, 325 life peers, 11 law lords, plus 26 bishops of the

Church of England. Less than 300 members attend regularly and most of them are life peers.

Main functions

☐ The Lords often tidy up Public Bills to make them more workable. They do not usually insist on amendments if the House of Commons rejects them.

☐ Some minor Bills start off in the Lords, to save time in the House of Commons.

☐ The Lords share the detailed work on Private Bills and delegated legislation.

☐ They debate general issues of the day.

☐ The House of Lords (or more accurately the Law Lords alone) is the supreme judicial court of appeal.

People have been talking about abolishing or reforming the House of Lords for many years. So far there has never been enough agreement in the House of Commons to give a majority to any particular proposals. The last attempt in 1968 collapsed through lack of backbench support.

A few countries, such as New Zealand, have only one House of Representatives, similar to our House of Commons. Most democratic countries have two Houses, both elected by the people. The American Senate (Upper House) represents the interests of the fifty States.

In the Republic of Ireland the Senate has similar functions to our House of Lords. The Senators are chosen by the Prime Minister, the Dáil (House of Commons), trade unions, industry, the Arts Council, and university graduates. The ruling party always has a majority in the Senate.

Our House of Lords always has a built-in majority of Conservative peers, and sometimes clashes head-on with Labour governments.

Chapter 13
The Government

'It's time *the Government* did something about it.' What do we mean? The whole apparatus of government? More likely we are thinking of the *executive* part of the system—the Ministers who make political decisions and see that they are carried out.

Her Majesty's Government

The Queen normally appoints as Prime Minister the Leader of the political party which has an overall majority of seats in the House of Commons. There is no law to say that she must, but there would be uproar if she didn't.

The Prime Minister chooses about 100 senior and junior Ministers, and the Queen formally appoints them. Collectively they are 'Her Majesty's Government'. You can find the current list in the first weekly edition of Hansard after a general election or after a reshuffle of Ministers.

The list always gives the names and titles in order of seniority and importance.

☐ *The Cabinet*—senior Ministers, with the Prime Minister first.

☐ *Ministers not in the Cabinet*—heads of minor government departments.

☐ *Junior Ministers*—Ministers of State, Parliamentary Secretaries and Under Secretaries, who are in charge of sections of big departments.

☐ *Law Officers*—four lawyers who handle government legal business.

☐ *Whips*—officially given ancient titles, such as 'Lords Commissioners of the Treasury'.

Most of these people are M.P.s and the rest are members of the House of Lords.

Coalition and minority Governments

What happens when the voters give no party an overall majority in the House of Commons? Fog covers the political scene, because there are no fixed rules.

The ordinary voter is apt to say, 'They ought to form a coalition Government, including the best men and women from all parties.' Commentators point out that coalitions are the rule, not the exception, in many democratic countries, notably Canada, West Germany, Holland and Belgium. Their voting systems are different and it is less likely for one party to get an overall majority.

But most British politicians hate coalition Governments and have willingly entered them only in wartime. Winston Churchill's coalition was already falling apart early in 1945 when the end of the war was in sight. His Ministers were facing the future and their ideas were poles apart. One Minister said privately, 'I had to bite my tongue when the bombs were falling, but I couldn't keep my mouth shut any longer when I knew we were safe.' Have you ever served on a committee which got nowhere fast, because the members disagreed fundamentally about what should be done?

The February 1974 general election gave no party an overall majority. The Conservative Prime Minister, Edward Heath, offered the Liberals some posts in his Government, but the Liberal Leader and M.P.s turned the offer down. Harold Wilson then formed a minority Labour government, which got a small majority in the October election. But by-election defeats turned it into a minority again by 1977. The new Prime Minister, James Callaghan, avoided a general election by making two agreements with the Liberal Leader, in March and July (Lib.–Lab. pacts). In return for Liberal M.P.s' support, he promised consultation on policies, especially about measures to reduce inflation.

On 25 May 1978 David Steel, the Liberal Leader, announced that the Lib.–Lab. pact would end in July. But the minority Labour Government continued with the support of Scottish National Party M.P.s. After the inconclusive Devolution Referendum the S.N.P. Members supported the Conservative vote of no confidence on 28 March 1979. The Government was defeated by 311 to 310 votes.

When a general election ends in stalemate we usually get a short-lived minority Government, as in 1924, 1929 and February 1974. The Ministers have to tread very carefully — defeat in the House of Commons on a vote of confidence means resignation. The Queen could then send for another party leader and ask him to form a Government. In practice she traditionally accepts the Prime Minister's request for a dissolution of Parliament and another general election.

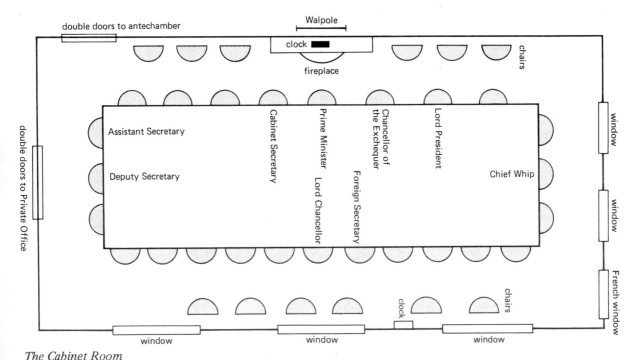

The Cabinet Room
(Source: 'The Cabinet', Patrick Gordon Walker, Jonathan Cape 1970)

The Cabinet

The Cabinet's main job is to make important decisions, after first weighing many sides of the questions. Parliament debates problems publicly and then takes a vote, for and against. The Cabinet discusses problems privately and tries to reach a unanimous decision; where this is not possible the Prime Minister 'collects voices' and declares the 'sense of the meeting'.

Prime Ministers used to include all Ministers who were heads of government departments. Now there are so many that some are left out, in order to keep the Cabinet small enough for real discussions— between sixteen and twenty-five members (See following table.)

Members of the Cabinet

Prime Minister, First Lord of the Treasury and Minister
    for the Civil Service
Lord President of the Council
Lord Chancellor
Chancellor of the Exchequer
Secretary of State for the Home Department
Secretary of State for Foreign and Commonwealth Affairs
Secretary of State for Education and Science
Paymaster General
Secretaries of State for
    Energy
    Industry
    Environment
    Northern Ireland
    Scotland
    Wales
    Defence
    Employment
    Social Services
Lord Privy Seal
Chief Secretary to the Treasury
Minister of Agriculture, Fisheries and Food
Secretary of State for Trade
Chancellor of the Duchy of Lancaster and Leader of
    the House of Commons
(*Source: Hansard, 9 May 1979*)

The Chief Whip is invited to Cabinet meetings, to advise on Parliamentary business and party reactions. Non-Cabinet Ministers and outside experts are sometimes invited, but only for particular items on the agenda.

The Cabinet Secretary is an important civil servant who attends all Cabinet meetings. His two assistants make notes and record the chief points of the discussion and the conclusions (decisions) in the Minutes.

104

Cabinet Meetings

The Cabinet meets at least once a week in the Cabinet Room at 10 Downing Street, the Prime Minister's official residence and office. If an emergency suddenly blows up, Cabinet Ministers can be hastily summoned without the usual written notice, wherever the Prime Minister happens to be.

Although Cabinet meetings are secret, you can learn something about Cabinet decisions from short statements to the press and from Ministers' speeches in Parliament. But how did they arrive at the decisions and what went on behind closed doors? Ex-Cabinet Ministers have lifted the veil of secrecy to some extent in books.

Patrick Gordon Walker's book *The Cabinet* (Jonathan Cape, 1970) is particularly illuminating. He gives an imaginary sample of the Minutes and two imaginary Cabinet debates. One of them is about a proposal to (1) put a tax on sweets (2) forbid advertising of sweets on TV and (3) issue free toothbrushes to school children. If you can get the book, notice the formal way in which the Prime Minister conducts the meeting, calls on Members to speak, gives his own views, and finally sums up the general conclusion.

Regular Cabinet meetings consider parliamentary business for the following week, a report from the Foreign Secretary, and any other items which the Prime Minister puts on the agenda. In 1967 Harold Wilson called a series of Cabinet meetings with only one item on the agenda—the Common Market. Edward Heath called at least one full-day discussion about long-term plans at Chequers, the Prime Minister's country residence.

Why does the Cabinet insist on secrecy? A very strong tradition of *collective responsibility* has developed. Once a conclusion has been reached it is binding on the whole Cabinet. Even if some members still disagree they must support it in public. (Do they tell their wives or just bottle it up?) If they simply cannot swallow the decision they resign and explain why in published letters and in Parliament. This convention of collective responsibility normally extends beyond the Cabinet to all the other Ministers outside. But the tradition occasionally breaks down. Labour Cabinet members and other Ministers were given a free vote in European Community debates in 1975 and 1977.

Cabinet Committees

The imaginary discussion about sweets and toothbrushes came to the Cabinet because a Cabinet Committee failed to agree. A lot of preparatory and detailed work is done in committees, chaired by the Prime Minister or other top-of-the-list Ministers. The Committees often make decisions which are reported to the Cabinet but not discussed there.

The Cabinet Committee system has grown like Jack's beanstalk since 1914, because Government business has grown. The Cabinet Secretariat keeps a list of something like seventy committees and sub-committees, but you will not find them in any reference book. We know that the Conservative Cabinet, 1970-4, had four major

105

committees—Defence and Overseas, Home Affairs, Emergency, and Legislation. The Prime Minister sets them up, closes temporary committees down, chooses the members and chairmen. Some committees include non-Cabinet Ministers and officials.

It is a flexible system and leaves the Cabinet free to concentrate on major problems which concern all departments, to make decisions when a committee cannot make up its collective mind, and to act as umpire when committees disagree with one another.

Wherever decisions are made, Cabinet Ministers have to explain and defend them in Parliament and in party and public meetings. It's a tough life, but as an American President once said, 'If you can't stand the heat, get out of the kitchen'.

The Prime Minister

A British Prime Minister has to be a master juggler, keeping a lot of plates spinning in the air at the same time. He needs the constitution of an ox, a first-class brain, outstanding political sense, and a long apprenticeship in the House of Commons. During this century Prime Ministers have served on average twenty-six years as an M.P. before they reached the top post.

You will already have noticed that a Prime Minister has a great deal of power.

☐ He chooses the Ministers and can sack them.

☐ Summons the Cabinet, decides its agenda, and carries great weight in its discussions.

☐ Uses his majority to get decisions through Parliament.

☐ Negotiates with foreign heads of government at summit meetings.

☐ Controls the civil service.

☐ Leads his party in Parliament and in the country.

☐ Decides the date of a general election.

☐ Speaks direct to the people on television and radio.

Only a Prime Minister knows to what extent he consults an 'Inner Cabinet' of close colleagues outside the normal machinery, and how far he relies on his own judgement.

In the past he was described as 'first among equals' in the Cabinet, but modern writers agree that he is now much more than that. Some say that he has become 'an elected monarch' or 'a sun around which planets revolve'.

Patrick Gordon Walker, who served in the Cabinets of two Prime Ministers, thinks differently. 'The truth is that the Cabinet and the party inside and outside Parliament do indeed find the Prime Minister an indispensable asset and that this gives him eminent power. But equally the Prime Minister cannot dispense with party, Parliament and Cabinet.'

He can be over-ruled in the Cabinet, and criticized by his own

Photo-quiz: British Prime Ministers since 1940; can you name them?

Answers:

1. Winston Churchill 1940-45; 2. Clement Attlee 1945-51; 3. Anthony Eden 1955-57; 4. Harold Macmillan 1957-63; 5. Alec Douglas-Home 1963-64; 6. Harold Wilson 1964-70, 1974-6; Edward Heath 1970-74; 8. James Callaghan 1976-9; 9. Margaret Thatcher 1979-.

back-bench M.P.s, as well as by the Opposition. Delegates at party conferences give him large pieces of their minds; he listens and argues back.

The Prime Minister tries to be the leader of the whole country. He keeps his ear to the ground, knowing that the people can kick him out by silently voting, however great his powers may be.

The Monarchy

Monarchy originally meant 'government by one person'. Nobody, least of all the Queen herself, imagines that she rules the country, as her ancestors used to do.

Constitutional lawyers draw up an impressive list of the monarch's political powers—the Royal Prerogative. Politicians say that these powers withered away before the Queen was born. It is a very long time since a monarch last refused the Royal Assent to a Bill, freely chose his own Ministers, or refused to dissolve Parliament. The Queen must now keep out of party politics and act on the advice of the Prime Minister. But government is still carried on in her name.

What part does the Queen play? As Head of State she receives

The Queen at her desk

and visits Presidents and Kings, presides at ceremonial functions, opens Parliament, formally appoints Ministers, judges, bishops and many lesser dignitaries. She reads and signs endless State papers and receives the Prime Minister's personal report once a week. She attends meetings of the Privy Council which announces approval of royal marriages, declarations of war, etc. and makes many other important decisions. (The Privy Council is a body with a long history; all Cabinet Ministers and other important persons become members and put P.C. after their names. Can you find out more about it and discover how it relates to the Cabinet?)

A boring job? Somebody has to do it. Would it be better done by an elected Head of State, perhaps like the President of West Germany? The United States constitution combines the roles of Head of State and Head of Government in one person—the President. In France the President is the real power in the land and his Prime Minister takes second place. Which system would you prefer?

You must have noticed that the Queen and Royal Family spend a lot of time on social duties—visiting all parts of the country and Commonwealth, opening new buildings, making and listening to speeches. The monarchy is hereditary and they are coached for the work almost from birth. One wonders if they find it a relief not to look good-humoured and interested when they are off duty.

Millions of people enjoy watching royal marriages and mourn when kings and queens die. They would probably agree that the Crown is a symbol of national unity, above and apart from Governments which come and go.

Chapter 14
Ministers, government departments and the civil service

If you could interview the Secretary of State for Education and Science, what would you ask him? 'Why do we take exams? Why don't we have enough books? Why was the school-leaving age raised to sixteen?'

He would probably reply that examinations are a matter for the school staff to decide; that the amount spent on books is decided by your local council and that some councils spend considerably more on books than others. But he would give a full answer to the third question, because the school-leaving age was raised by a Government Order under the Education Act, 1944. Like all Ministers, his main concern is broad national policy.

The work of a Minister

Here is an imaginary interview with an Education Minister, based on real answers which Ministers have given to questions about their work.

What is your main job as a Minister? Helping to make important decisions on Government policy, as part of the Cabinet team, and taking responsibility for the way relevant decisions are carried out in my department. For example, if the Cabinet decides on a universal comprehensive system for secondary schools, I carry the can for making that policy a reality.

What do you do in your office at the department? Mainly paper work, discussions and making decisions. Suppose a metropolitan district council sends us a very unusual plan for reorganising its colleges of further education. My officials prepare a file of papers which they call a 'case'. It includes their summary of points for and against the plan, as well as the plan itself. I read the lot, discuss it with my political colleagues and senior officials, and probably with deputations of councillors and their officials, and delegates from the technical teachers' trade union and from the National Union of Students. After all that I must make up my mind—approve or reject the plan, or accept it provided some changes are made. Whatever I decide somebody won't like it.

The officials also 'brief' me with papers for Cabinet and Cabinet Committee meetings, drafts of answers to questions in Parliament, background information for speeches and discussions with deputations. Together with answering and signing letters it adds up to mounds of paper every day. I can't get through it all in my offices in the department and in the House of Commons. I take the rest home in the evenings and try to clear it, working quietly till midnight or later.

Who are these officials you talk about? Most of them are senior civil servants. The Permanent Secretary is the top official in the department and my chief adviser; I see him at least half-an-hour almost every day. The Deputy Secretaries are concerned with big sections, such as further education. And I sometimes see Under-Secretaries who prepare a lot of the cases.

110

My Private Secretary is a young official lower down the ladder. He arranges my appointments, organizes most of my correspondence (with the help of assistants and typists), sieves the telephone calls, and accompanies me like a shadow until I go home. He will probably become a Permanent or Deputy Secretary one day. I also see the department's Press Officer about publicity for my speeches and main policy decisions.

What do you mean by 'political colleagues'? The Minister of State and two Parliamentary Secretaries chosen by the Prime Minister for this department. They take a lot of work off my shoulders and we discuss unusual problems and things which might cause a political outcry. I also have an unpaid Parliamentary Private Secretary, a young M.P. who helps to keep me in touch with our own back-benchers.

Can you describe your work in the Cabinet and Cabinet Committees? No! But you can read all about it in thirty years' time when the records will be open to the public.

Do you ever get out of London? Oh yes. As a Minister I open new schools and colleges and attend educational conferences and exhibitions. Apart from formal speeches, I usually have to talk to the top brass and I wish there were more opportunities to chat with rank-and-file teachers and pupils.

Do you spend much time in Parliament? Not as much as when I was a back-bencher or an Opposition Front Bench spokesman. Like any M.P. I'm in the Chamber for the Prime Minister's statements and leading speeches in the main debates. And, of course, for three-line whip divisions, which may take place at ten o'clock two or three times a week. I often work in my office at the House in the afternoons and evenings—more papers and discussions. I even sleep there occasionally during all-night sittings. When I'm lucky I go home about seven or eight o'clock.

How often do you answer M.P.s' questions? My turn to answer oral questions comes up about once in three weeks, twenty or thirty questions at a time. As you know, the answers are prepared by my officials, but I check them and have to cope with tricky supplementaries. I give Written Answers to any oral questions which we don't have time to reach.

What happens when there's a new Education Bill? It becomes my major task, once the Cabinet has settled the main ideas. It's a huge departmental team job at every stage. I have to present the White Paper to the Cabinet and also explain it in the House of Commons. I approve the final draft of the Bill, make the main Second Reading speech on its principles, steer it through Standing Committee (deciding which amendments to accept), and finally present it to the House again at the Report Stage and Third Reading.

All this involves months of discussions with political colleagues, senior officials, outside bodies (such as teachers' trade unions and

Extract from Hansard, Written Answers, 21 March 1974. See also School-leaving Dates Act on page 96

School Leaving Age

Mr. Clemitson asked the Secretary of State for Education and Science if he will seek powers to allow 16-year-old pupils to leave school, if they so desire, on completion of their examinations, without waiting for the end of the summer term.

Mr. Armstrong : My right hon. Friend will be studying the opinions, which are being sought at present, of the teacher and local authority associations on the proposal for an early summer leaving date.

Student Grants

Mr. Rooker asked the Secretary of State for Education and Science if he will make a statement concerning his policy towards the abolition of the system of parental contributions in student grants.

Mr. Gerry Fowler : This is one of the matters being considered in the current review of student grants. My right hon. Friend hopes to announce the results of the review within about the next two months.

111

local councils), and endless memoranda and drafts. Any Minister is heartily glad when a Bill reaches port. But after that come new rules and regulations (Statutory Instruments), some of which I may have to defend in Parliament or from attacks by outside bodies, in spite of all the previous consultations.

What about your constituency work as an M.P.?   I get even more letters than I used to do as a back-bencher. I hold surgeries on one Saturday morning a month, from 10 a.m. until noon, but they always over-run the time. People say that a Minister is a god in his department. In his surgery he is very much down to earth, trying to help fellow human beings. I pay my own secretary to deal with constituency correspondence, including invitations to local functions and to meet pressure groups and deputations.

Mrs Thatcher (the first woman to become leader of a British political party) receives a deputation

What about your party?   As a Minister I'm concerned with how and when to put party ideas into practice. Sometimes I have to compromise because there are practical limits on what one can do. I'd like to get rid of every obsolete school building, but other services need money too, and people will take only so much taxation, even if there were enough skilled building workers.

I meet our back-benchers at the House of Commons and attend the annual party conference. I try to fit in the main meetings of my constituency party, and I have a chat with the chairman and secretary after Saturday surgeries.

What a life!   Yes, one lives at top pressure. But there's real satisfaction in doing something to shape the future.

Government departments

When people talk about 'Whitehall' they mean either the wide road

The main Government Departments 1981

Department	Minister in charge	Responsibilities
H.M. Treasury	Chancellor of the Exchequer	Finance, national economy, control of current and capital spending of government departments.
Foreign and Commonwealth Office	Foreign Secretary	Diplomatic Service, representing U.K. and protecting British subjects abroad. Overseas Development Administration.
Home Office	Home Secretary	Law and order; police, prison and probation services; fire services; aliens, immigration, race relations: explosives, firearms, drugs, poisons.
Department of Employment	Secretary for Employment	Employment services (local employment offices/ job centres); training services; industrial relations; factory inspection.
Department of Industry	Secretary of State for Industry	Policy for industry including small firms; regional policy and financial assistance; relations with public industries.
Department of Energy	Secretary of State for Energy	Fuel and power supplies: oil, coal, gas, electricity, nuclear energy.
Department of Trade	Secretary of State for Trade	Commercial policy and overseas relations; exports; information; consumer affairs.
Department of Transport	Minister for Transport	Public transport industries; motorways and trunk roads; safety and licensing.
Department of Health and Social Security	Secretary of State for Social Services	National Health Service; social services run by local councils; social security benefits and pensions.
Department of the Environment	Secretary of State for Environment	Local government and development; housing and construction; roads and transport; environmental pollution; public buildings and works; planning.
Ministry of Defence	Secretary of State for Defence	Administration of armed forces; defence policy.
Department of Education and Science	Secretary of State for Education and Science	Schools, further and higher education; civil scientific research; libraries and museums; the Arts.
Ministry of Agriculture, Fisheries and Food	Minister for Agriculture	Policies to improve efficiency of these industries; food supplies and storage.
Scottish Office	Secretary of State for Scotland	These departments are responsible for some of the above services in the areas named together with a special concern for their development in the special circumstances of Scotland, Wales or Northern Ireland. They are also concerned with problems and issues arising within their particular areas.
Welsh Office	Secretary of State for Wales	
Northern Ireland	Secretary of State for Northern Ireland	

The Foreign and Commonwealth Office, King Charles Street, off Whitehall

leading down to Parliament Square in London, or the whole apparatus of government departments. A few departments still line the road; most of them are now scattered over London.

There are about thirty departments. Every Prime Minister chops and changes them. For example, Harold Wilson merged the Ministry of Power with his Department of Technology in 1969. Edward Heath moved it to his Department of Trade and Industry in 1971, then separated it again in 1974 as the Ministry of Energy, after the oil crises of 1973. The table on page 113 shows the departmental structure approved by Mrs. Thatcher in 1979. The Treasury remains the most powerful department, because it keeps tight control over the spending of all the other departments.

The departments' functions vary a great deal. The Department of Health and Social Security and the Department of Employment need large outside staffs in regional and local offices. Most of the Foreign Office staff are stationed all over the world. When local councils run a public service, like education, the Department is concentrated in its London headquarters.

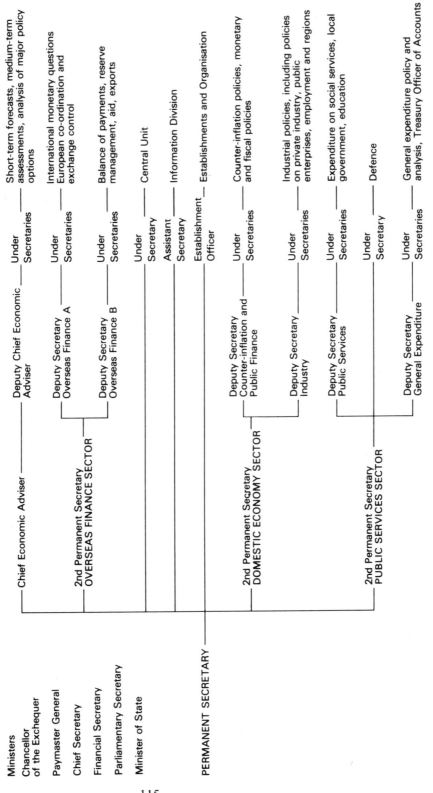

How a government department is organized (The Treasury)
(Source: Her Majesty's Treasury, HMSO, 1976)

The exact organization of each department depends on its functions. They follow a similar broad pattern, with the political Ministers at the top, then the senior civil servants, with the rest of the officials and staff working under their directions. The political heads come and go with changes in Government. The officials stay put, serving whichever Government is in power. They change their jobs when they are promoted or moved sideways, though usually in the same department.

In 1981 there were about 700 000 civil servants. About 240 000 are employed by the Ministry of Defence. About three-quarters of all civil servants work outside London in regional and local offices. The Government plans to reduce the total number to 630 000 by 1984.

'Ministerial responsibility' can mean two things — the collective responsibility of Ministers for Cabinet decisions, and the responsibility of each Minister for the actions of his own department. When mistakes come to light he must defend his staff in Parliament if they have carried out orders or followed clear lines of policy. If the mistakes or delays are serious the Minister must explain and apologize, or even resign.

Some years ago there was a case in which two men were wrongly imprisoned, one of them for five years. The Home Secretary told the House of Commons (8 April 1974) that he had ordered a thorough investigation of identity parades, and that the men had been released and would be financially compensated. He did not say what would happen to the junior official who had neglected Mr Virag's case in 1971—probably a severe reprimand and loss of promotion.

Can you discover any other instances where a government department has blundered badly?

The Civil Service

Civil servants are employees of the central government. Most people meet some of the lower ranks when they enquire locally about income tax, benefits, pensions, and job vacancies. Very few people meet the senior civil servants who advise Ministers and help to work out policy.

The chart on page 117 shows the main grades in the Home Civil Service. In addition there are many specialists, such as doctors, lawyers, economists, scientists, engineers and architects. About 157 000 'industrial' civil servants include skilled craftsmen, cleaners, canteen assistants — the employees one finds in any big organization.

In the main Administration Group there are ten grades from Clerical Assistant up to Assistant Secretary. Your school careers library probably has pamphlets about Clerical Assistants, Clerical Officers, Executive Officers, and many other posts in the civil service. The pamphlets will give you the latest details about the kind of work they do, pre-entry qualifications, opportunities for promotion, training schemes and day-release courses.

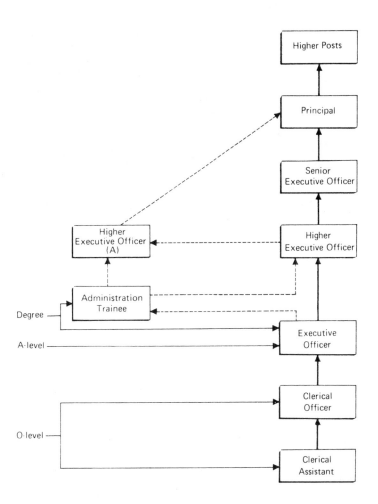

Structure of the administration group of the Civil Service.
(Source: 'Executive Careers: Posts in Government Service', Civil Service Commission, January 1972)

A lot of the work has to be learnt by doing it, under supervision. Every civil servant learns to keep careful records, refer to codes of regulations, and pass anything doubtful up to his immediate senior (who may pass it on, like a hot potato, to his senior).

Every entrant is told to follow a strict code of honesty. 'An officer must not accept any gift or reward from any member of the public or organization with whom he is brought into contact by reason of his official duties.' The occasional black sheep is front page news.

Civil servants are traditionally cautious in their relations with Parliament and the public. There are good reasons for this:

☐ The strict Official Secrets Act imposes close restrictions on the sharing or passing of information.

☐ Tremors go through a whole section when an M.P. asks a Parliamentary Question about its (alleged) slip-ups.

☐ The Public Accounts Committee examines the accounts of each department in turn and questions the Permanent Secretary and other

Photo-quiz: Can you say what are the occupations of these Civil Service employees?

Answers: 1. Machine operator (computer); 2. Assistant Scientific Officer (Laboratory of the Government Chemist); 3. Clerical officer - Supplementary Benefits; 4. Sheet metal work apprentice at Royal Aircraft Establishment; 5. Field surveyors; 6. Assistant Preventive Officer (Customs and Excise).

senior staff. (See page 124.) Its findings are reported to Parliament. Other Select Committees scrutinize the work of the departments (see Chapter 12).

☐ The Ombudsman (Parliamentary Commissioner) tracks down people's complaints about civil servants, handed on to him by M.P.s. He can demand to see the dustiest file and reports any maladministration to Parliament. Inland Revenue officers seem to get more angry clients than other departments and have been rapped on the knuckles for long delays in making income tax repayments. All this stems from the doctrine of ministerial responsibility.

How good is the Civil Service? It has the proud reputation of being the best in the world—efficient, politically neutral, incorruptible, a true public service.

Its best friends would not call it perfect. Ordinary people sometimes grumble about officials who seem to treat them as fiddlers or layabouts, or assume that they understand the complicated jargon of regulations. Civil servants, in unguarded moments off duty, say rude things about us, the public, and wonder how they keep their patience.

The Fulton Committee (1968) recommended improvements in organization, recruitment, training and promotion. More flexibility, less secrecy, and more contact between higher civil servants and the outside world. Some of the committee's suggestions have been put into effect by the new Civil Service Department, and changes are still going on.

Ministers grumble about the power of the Mandarins (their nickname for senior civil servants) to hold up radical changes in policy. 'I entered the Ministry bursting with new ideas and asked for their comments', said a Minister. 'Two months later they handed me bulging files, explaining very clearly why nothing could be done.' Determined Ministers like Winston Churchill and Ernest Bevin used to tell the Mandarins to try again and use their fine brains to work out how things could be done.

Sir William Armstrong was interviewed on television just before he retired as Head of the Home Civil Service. 'I have a very strong suspicion that governments are nothing like as important as they think they are, and that the ordinary work of making things and moving things about . . . is so much more important than what the Government does that the Government can make enormous mistakes and we can still survive.'

Interviewer — 'As long as we have our Civil Service'.

Sir William Armstrong — 'No, no. Even in spite of it'.

(The Listener. 28 March 1974.)

Chapter 15
Public finance

Public spending (by central government, local authorities and public corporations) adds up to about half our total national output. The national income and expenditure planned for 1980-81 is shown on the tables below.

We all share in the raising of the money and benefit from the spending. The bulk of the income comes from taxation. Nobody likes paying taxes, but at the same time we often protest that 'they' ought to spend more money on schools, pensions, sports facilities, or other things.

Some of the benefits we get are 'collective', such as protection by the police and armed services. Most people on balance receive more from public spending when they are young, old, sick or unemployed, and contribute more when they are able-bodied and working.

The Government's
Expenditure Plans 1980–81

Planned government expenditure, 1980-81

	£ million
Defence	8,062
Overseas aid and other overseas services:	
Overseas aid	782
EEC contributions	1,000
Other overseas services	409
Agriculture, fisheries, food and forestry	993
Industry, energy, trade and employment	2,870
Government lending to nationalised industries	900
Roads and Transport	2,914
Housing	5,078
Other environmental services	3,213
Law, order and protective services	2,542
Education and science, arts and libraries	9,246
Health and personal social services	9 194
Social security	19,289
Other public services	997
Common services	1,088
Northern Ireland	2,150
Total	70,729

(*Source: 'The Government's Expenditure Plans 1980-81', HMSO, 1981*)

Taxation and other receipts, 1980-81	
	£ million
	1980-81
	Budget Forecast
Taxation	
Inland Revenue:	
Income tax	23,830
Surtax	8
Corporation tax	4,860
Petroleum revenue tax	2,560
Capital gains tax	490
Development land tax	25
Estate duty	17
Capital transfer tax	400
Stamp duties	670
Total Inland Revenue	32,860
Customs and Excise:	
Value added tax	12,450
Oil	3,650
Tobacco	2,775
Spirits, beer, wine, cider and perry	2,825
Betting and gaming	475
Car tax	575
Other excise duties	10
European Community own resources	
Customs duties, etc	950
Agricultural levies	290
Total Customs and Excise	24,000
Vehicle excise duties	1,411
National insurance surcharge	3,509
Total Taxation	61,780
Miscellaneous Receipts:	
Broadcast receiving licences	535
Interest and dividends	300
Other	2,800
Total	65,415

Central Government finance—The Budget

In the spring, at the beginning of the Government's financial year, the Chancellor of the Exchequer presents his annual Budget to the House of Commons. It is a financial statement about the past year, Government intentions for the coming year, and changes in taxation.

The original aim of the Budget was just to raise money for Government spending. Since the 1940s it has become one of the Government's main tools in managing the whole economy, and in altering the distribution of income and wealth between different groups of people.

The Chancellor of the Exchequer starts his long budget speech with a review of the economy and particular economic problems, such as inflation, balance of payments, unemployment. Only after this are the details of tax changes etc. revealed.

Currently Britain, like other industrialized countries, is suffering from problems of inflation and economic recession. The Budget forms an important part of the Government's strategy for dealing with these difficult problems. There is no straightforward solution and even the experts cannot agree on what should be done. A given change may provide a short-term solution to one problem but in doing so create another. Whatever the general approach the Opposition party is likely to favour an alternative strategy and both can easily be proved wrong in their forecasts. From time to time it will be necessary to make adjustments during the course of the financial year and when this is the case a 'supplementary' budget or 'mini-Budget' is presented.

The Government spends about two-thirds of all public expenditure, but raises three-quarters of all public revenue. Why the difference? The Budget includes money which is passed on to local councils in grants, and to public corporations for about half their 'capital investment' in new buildings and machinery.

Taxes

Central government taxes used to be classified as direct or indirect—income tax is paid direct to the tax collectors, V.A.T. is paid indirectly through shopkeepers and others. Nowadays they are usually divided into three groups—taxes on income, expenditure, and capital (or wealth). All taxes are paid into the 'Consolidated Fund', which pays the money out to government departments.

1. Taxes on income

Income tax   is the biggest single revenue raiser, paid by most of the working population and by some retired people. You can find out the current rates of tax and allowances by borrowing the Inland

(Source: Financial Statement and Budget Report 1980-81 as presented in 'Britain 1981: An Official Handbook' HMSO, 1981)

Revenue notes which are sent to everybody who pays income tax. (You will probably need help to understand them.) Economists call it a 'progressive' tax, that is, the larger a taxpayer's income, the larger the proportion which he pays in tax.

Corporation tax   is paid by companies out of their profits.

National Insurance contributions   are sometimes classified as a tax on income, because they come out of the pay packet. Employees pay them along with income tax, under the Pay-As-You-Earn (PAYE) procedure.

2. *Taxes on expenditure*

These are 'regressive' taxes, that is, the larger a taxpayer's income, the smaller the proportion he pays in tax. If the tax on twenty cigarettes is 15p, how will it work out for two men with different earnings, say £30 and £60 a week, if both smoke 100 cigarettes a week?

Value Added Tax   is levied on nearly all goods and services. The main exceptions are food, books and exports. (Sweets, ice-cream and soft drinks were taxed by the 1974 Budget.) VAT is collected at all stages from producer to retailer and finally settles on us, the consumers. There are heavy taxes on petrol, tobacco and alcoholic drinks, calculated on the quantities people buy—a gallon of petrol, an ounce of tobacco, a bottle of spirits.

Customs duties   are levied at the ports on certain goods entering the country.

Taxes on expenditure are big revenue raisers. They also raise prices, but we probably notice these taxes less than the very clear Pay-As-You-Earn income tax figure on pay-slips.

3. *Taxes on capital (or wealth)*

In this sense 'wealth' can take the form of land, stocks and shares, houses and other property, antiques, jewellery, paintings and so on. (Some of these things produce 'unearned income' for the owners, on which they pay income tax.)

Death duties   started in the late nineteenth century—'Pay-As-You-Die'. They have not altered the distribution of wealth very much, because ways were found to avoid them legally. New kinds of taxes on wealth, gifts and inheritance, have become an important issue between the political parties.

Estate Duty was replaced by Capital Transfer Tax in 1975. This tax applies broadly to gifts of personal wealth, whether they are made during a person's lifetime or on his death.

Government borrowing—The National Debt

Governments borrow a lot of money, especially in wartime. At the end of the Second World War the National Debt was £23 000 millions. By 1973 the total accumulated debt had risen to £36 000 millions. By 1980 it was estimated at £93 330 millions.

The segmental diagram on the next page shows that the main

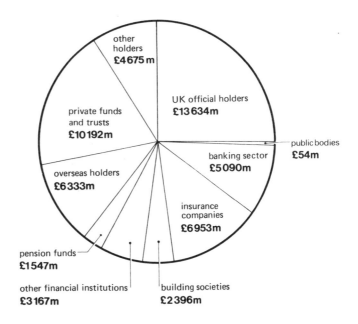

Who holds the National Debt? (In million £)
Estimated distribution at 31 March 1976 (total: £54 041 million)
(Source: Bank of England Quarterly Bulletin, June 1977)

lenders are people and organizations within the country. Most of the 'overseas holders' are foreign central banks and international bodies such as the International Monetary Fund.

'UK official holders' means in effect that the Government lends money to itself! The huge amounts collected by the National Insurance Fund and by National and Trustee Savings Banks are invested in government securities (stocks), where they earn interest.

'Private funds and trusts' include millions of people who put their spare money into National Savings. They keep the certificates and eventually cash them.

Most government securities are bought and sold through stockbrokers. You can find a list of them on the financial page of any newspaper, with the current price, the fixed rate of interest, and in some cases the year when the Government will have to redeem (pay back) the debt.

The National Loans Fund uses this borrowed money (1) to make loans to local councils and public corporations (2) to make up any deficit in the Consolidated Fund, when taxes are not enough to cover government expenditure.

The National Debt is an ingenious way of raising enormous sums of money apart from taxation. But the taxpayers have to foot the bill for paying interest on all these debts.

The House of Commons as financial watchdog

The Government cannot raise or spend money without the approval of the House of Commons. The principle that 'redress of grievances must precede supply' goes right back to the time of the Normans. The House of Commons is supposed to hold 'the power of the purse' but how strong this power really is is a matter which has been much discussed.. Several avenues are open to M.P.s in their efforts to exercise financial control.

Proposals for raising money

The Budget is presented by the Chancellor of the Exchequer in March or April. The House of Commons legalizes any immediate tax changes (for example 'another twopence on a pint of beer from midnight') by passing 'Budget Resolutions'. Then the House gets down to long debates on the *Finance Bill*, which includes all the Budget proposals and must be passed by the first week in August. Major changes in the Government's proposals are not frequent but in 1978 changes were made in those for income tax. In 1981 a number of Conservative M.P.s threatened to vote against the sizeable increase in the price of petrol but the Chancellor made only a small concession on the price of diesel fuel.

'Supply' Days

On twenty-nine days in the Partliamentary session the Opposition has the right to choose the subject for debate. Originally the theory was that it was Government spending which was being discussed in this way but these debates are no longer directly linked to spending. Sometimes financial matters are directly discussed but more often it is the general policies which are debated. Financial matters may be raised at Question Time, on Private Members' Motions and on the Adjournment Debate (see Chapter 12). Reference has also been made to the important system of Select Committees which was set up in 1979. The hope of many M.P.s and others is that these will prove to be more effective than was the Expenditure Committee which they succeeded. (Keep your eye on the newspapers for reports of their work.)

Post-mortem control

The powerful *Public Accounts Committee* examines closely how government departments have already spent money in the previous year. This committee has fifteen M.P.s and is always chaired by the Opposition's leading financial expert. The examination is very thorough because the committee is assisted by the Comptroller and Auditor General and his expert staff of 600. The Comptroller is appointed by the House of Commons, not by the Government. One might ask, 'What's the use if the money has already been spent?' Two answers—the Public Accounts Committee keeps departments on their toes and sometimes finds things under the financial carpet. In March 1973 the Committee reported that the choicest parts of the

MPs propose new grant system for over 16-year-olds

By Our Political Staff

A new system of grants for children who stay on at school after 16 is recommended by an all-party committee of MPs today, — and the MPs says that part of the grant should go direct to the children, instead of to their parents.

The recommendations are made in a report from a sub-committee of the influential Commons Expenditure Committee.

The MPs say that a uniform national system to help less well-off families keep their children at school would be in the national interest.

Many local authorities already help poorer children to stay on at school, but the amounts they pay vary considerably. "A family living in one town may find themselves treated far less generously than their counterparts in an adjacent town," says the report.

The MPs say that "Every witness decried the unfairness of this system and we agree that allowances should now be calculated in accordance with a national scale."

Replace

They recommend:
● All existing allowances available to 16 to 18 year-old schoolchildren, including free school meals, should be scrapped and replaced by a single educational maintenance allowance.
● The allowance should be the same all over the country, though run by local authorities for the benefit of families in financial need. Those who now qualify for free school meals would qualify for the full sum.
● It would be paid in confidence, in a lump sum and at regular intervals, with one third going direct to the child and two thirds to the parents. "By the age of 16, children nowadays expect to make many decisions for themselves. We think this change should be reflected in the way allowances are paid."
● To make sure that public money is not wasted, every school should have the right to expel a pupil over 16 for lack of effort.
● The new educational maintenance allowance should be available from September next year.

North Sea had been let to companies on very generous terms, on licences which would run for forty-six years without revision. This report made the Government sit up and promise to look into oil and gas licences again.

The Government is responsible for financial policy. The House of Commons is a hairy watchdog, sniffing at its heels and sometimes nipping them.

Chapter 16
The Smiths and democracy

In Chapter 1 we met the Smith family, concerned about their personal problems and getting help from public services. They take their democratic rights for granted. 'We don't take a lot of interest in government and politics. We always vote at general elections, sometimes at local elections, and that's about it.'

The Smiths play a bigger part in government than they realize. They certainly use their right of free speech and their freedom to join organizations—which contribute something to the community and quite often influence local councils and the Government.

Jack Smith is a member of a trade union, pays his weekly dues, occasionally goes to branch meetings, and takes his working grievances to the shop steward. He knows that an organized body of workers has much more influence on the Government than the same individuals acting separately.

He is also a member of the District Allotments Society, which buys seeds and fertilizers in bulk and organizes flower and vegetable shows. Two years ago the local council talked about using the allotment land for building. The Society objected strongly, sent a deputation to the Town Hall, wrote to the local newspaper and M.P., and won.

Margaret Smith is on the committee of the Residents' Association. It started last year when people on the estate got fed up with vandalism. First, they complained to the police; then they asked the local council to provide more sports facilities where the lads could work off their energy. They met a councillor who believed in 'grass roots democracy', helped them to organize the Association, and urged his fellow councillors to let them take over part of the management of the estate. He said, 'Why not let the people who live there decide the priorities? Repairs, painting, sites for play areas, bus stops—let them sort it out'.

Mrs Jones belongs to the Pensioners' Club which runs weekly meetings and trips. The club members have helped the Social Services Department of the council to make a list of old and disabled people who live alone. Elizabeth's Youth Club uses the list, too; they have organized working parties to help with gardening, shopping, decorating and odd jobs.

There is another kind of democracy which hardly exists for the Smiths. No manager at work asks Jack Smith if he can think of a better way of doing his job. Margaret Smith has ideas about better service for customers at the shop where she works part-time, but that is considered to be none of her business.

The political parties are talking about 'industrial democracy', which means having a real say in what goes on at work. Or at least an opportunity to be consulted direct or through elected representatives, whether the ownership is public or private.

Democracy, political or industrial, is often slow and tiresome, as anybody who has served on committees will tell you. Endless arguments before decisions are made, vital changes held up. But 'government by the people' is very much more likely to produce 'government for the people' than any other system. We know where the shoe pinches.

126

Sources of information

General

1 The following reference books are published annually
   Whitaker's Almanac
   The Municipal Year Book
   Annual Abstract of Statistics, HMSO.
2 The political parties publish cheap, factual and up-to-date handbooks about local government, local and parliamentary elections, as well as policy leaflets and pamphlets.
   Conservative Party—Conservative Political Centre, 32 Smith Square, London, SW1P 3HH.
   Labour Party—144-152 Walworth Road, London, SE17 1JT.
   Liberal Party—Liberal Party Organization, 1 Whitehall Place, London SW1A 2HE.
   Social Democratic Party—4 Cowley Street, London SW1.
3 Official Reports, published by HMSO.
   Management of Local Government, Vol. 1. 1967. (Maud Management Report.)
   Report on the Home Civil Service, 1968. (Fulton Report.)
   Report of the Royal Commission on Local Government in England, 1969. (Maud Report.)
   The New Local Authorities: Management and Structure, 1972. (Bains Report.)
   Report of the Royal Commission on the Constitution, 1973. (Kilbrandon Report.)
4 Information on aspects of Parliament suitable for school use is available from the Education Officer, Public Information Office, House of Commons, London SW1A 0AA.

Local Government

1 The most useful sources for local projects, wall newspapers etc. are the Information Offices of district and county councils, local newspapers and libraries.
2 NALGO (National and Local Government Officers' Association). Local branch secretaries of the union arrange loans from the London H.Q. library of films, books, wall panels, pamphlets and so on. Some branches lend their own visual and aural aids about local government.

Further Information

1 Central Office of Information, Hercules Road, London SE1 7DU. The Reference Division issues a sales list of reference documents, including short, cheap pamphlets about government, social services and so on. The Photographs Division sells photographs and photoposters. The Circulation Section supplies free publications, for example *Economic Progress Report*, with good diagrams.
2 Central Film Library, Government Building, Bromyard Avenue, Acton, London W3 7JB. Lends films and sells filmstrips on government and citizenship.

3 Hansard Society, 16 Gower Street, London WC1, has an information service about Parliament. (Public reference libraries have copies of the weekly Hansard.)

4 Electoral Reform Society, 6 Chancel Street, Southwark, London SE1 0UX, publishes leaflets and pamphlets about proportional representation.

5 Professional Associations.

The Politics Association exists to promote the study and teaching of politics and government in schools. For details of membership and publications available write to: Mrs J. Prout, 14 Wakefield Close, Strood, Rochester, Kent, ME2 2RL.

Other associations with an interest in the topics covered in this book include:

The Economics Association, 16 Cedar Road, Sutton, Surrey, SM2 5DF; Association for the Teaching of the Social Sciences— Lorraine Judge, Allandale, Johnshill, Lochwinnoch, Renfrewshire.

6 Books. The following will be found useful by young people for reading, reference and 'dipping into':

The BBC Guide to Parliament, BBC in association with *House Magazine*, 1979.

The Guardian Directory of Pressure Groups, Wilton House Publications, 1976.

Des Wilson, *So You Want to be Prime Minister*, Penguin Books, 1979.

Andrew Phillips, *The Living Law*, Clearway, 1976.